THE BEAUTY SUIT

The Beauty Suit

HOW MY YEAR OF *RELIGIOUS MODESTY* *MADE ME A* *BETTER FEMINIST*

Lauren Shields

BEACON PRESS, BOSTON

BEACON PRESS
Boston, Massachusetts
www.beacon.org

Beacon Press books
are published under the auspices of
the Unitarian Universalist Association of Congregations.

21 20 19 18   8 7 6 5 4 3 2 1

This book is printed on acid-free paper that meets the uncoated paper
ANSI/NISO specifications for permanence as revised in 1992.

Text design and composition by Kim Arney

Bible quotations are from the New Revised Standard Version Bible,
copyright © 1989 National Council of the Churches of Christ
in the United States of America. Used by permission.
All rights reserved worldwide.

Quotations from the Qur'an are from Sumbul Ali-Karamali,
The Muslim Next Door: The Qur'an, the Media, and That Veil Thing
(Ashland, OR: White Cloud Press, 2008), which draws alternately
from translations of Muhammad Asad and A. J. Arberry.

Library of Congress Cataloging-in-Publication Data

Names: Shields, Lauren, author.
Title: The beauty suit : how my year of religious modesty made me
a better feminist / Lauren Shields.
Description: Boston : Beacon Press, 2018. | Includes bibliographical
references and index.
Identifiers: LCCN 2017042211 (print) | LCCN 2017050874 (ebook) |
ISBN 9780807093931 (ebook) | ISBN 9780807093924 (pbk. : alk. paper)
Subjects: LCSH: Modesty—Religious aspects—Christianity. | Feminism—Religious
aspects—Christianity. | Feminism. | Women—Identity. | Sex role. |
Feminine beauty (Aesthetics)
Classification: LCC BV4647.M63 (ebook) | LCC BV4647.M63 S55 2018 (print) |
DDC 241/.4—dc23
LC record available at https://lccn.loc.gov/2017042211

For Mom, my first love;
And for Less. You were right. Shut up.

CONTENTS

INTRODUCTION

WOMEN CAN DO ANYTHING —
NO, NOT THAT

ATLANTA, JULY 2013

I stare at the screen, my head in my hands, peering over the tops of my fingers in shock. "What is everyone so *mad* about?" I moan.

For the nine months leading up to my thirtieth birthday, I'd covered my hair, arms, and legs and stopped wearing makeup. I called my project the Modesty Experiment, and I'd published a blog about it to stay accountable. I'd written about it for *Salon*, and the reaction was . . . mixed.

Admittedly, I should have worded some things more carefully. I'd called a young girl in a hijab who had inspired me "half Muslim." That was dumb; I meant half Iranian. No one is half Muslim. Plus, I'd used the phrase "dressing like a Quaker" when I meant "dressing like a Quaker from 1695." I deserved the flak I caught for those.

What hurts are the grammatically correct paragraphs, in the comments section and via a flood of email, that amount to lots and lots of people saying, "How dare you imply that a covered woman might not be oppressed? You should be ashamed of yourself," and, "You're supporting misogynistic Islamist ideology with your project. By doing this, you are hurting women everywhere." My

1

loudest detractors are other women, most of whom are self-avowed feminists. Somehow, by covering my hair, arms, and legs for several months and claiming that doing so was liberating, I seem to have transgressed a sacred cultural boundary. I also seem to have implied that women *should* cover up, because it was somehow "better."

But that was never my intention. I had experimented with re-ligiously inspired modesty—you might say I veiled temporarily—because I found it to be a way to resist the idea that a woman's worth, and her power in the world, primarily depend upon being beautiful. Also, I hadn't done it to prove a point to others; I'd done it because it had become abundantly clear to me that, although I saw myself as a liberated woman, I believed in my bones that what made me worthwhile was my ability to squeeze myself into what I would come to call the Beauty Suit.

This belief is not anomalous among women, as I learned during my experiment. It's also not mere vanity. Vanity is unseemly because how one looks is supposed to be unimportant, and obsession with something so frivolous is worthy of ridicule. But the truth is that women receive the message that nothing is more important than looking good, every single day of our lives. Beauty, we are told, is anything but frivolous.

Though I suspect most women know what I mean when I say the "Beauty Suit," let me make it clearer. Fitting satisfactorily into the Beauty Suit is not just about a woman's genes; it's also about her willingness to make her body available to be looked at. A woman must not only be young, pale, and thin but also wear a costume when she leaves the house, one partly based on satisfying the male gaze. (I hate that I have to use such a Women's Studies 101 phrase, but when it stops being a thing, maybe we can finally fucking retire it.) Uncovered, stylish, "done" hair; makeup that's expensive and time-consuming but considered tasteless when there's "too much"; clothing that hugs our bodies and exposes our arms, legs, and sometimes stomachs and backs; shoes that are agonizing to wear and expensive to own but are somehow near mandatory for professional wear; these are the components of the Beauty Suit.

The Beauty Suit takes our bodies as they naturally exist and adds enormous amounts of money, time, and effort, in quantities that men are never expected to approach (and in fact are sometimes made fun of if they appear to). A woman's worth is judged by how perfectly she fulfills the so-called requirements of beauty. But even if she does not fulfill them—because she is over forty, let's say, or carries more weight than is considered ideal—she is still expected to wear the Suit. In fact, she must try harder, and if she does not, she is accused of the worst sin of womanhood: being a slob.

We know all this is hard, expensive, and ultimately unnecessary in the hunter-gatherer sense. We know beauty is oppressive and narrow and exhausting. And yet many women pursue it anyway. Why?

Because being willing to wear the Suit has become a prerequisite for empowerment. Women cannot possibly be liberated if we are not wearing it. Conversely, and perhaps more damaging, many of us have come to accept hotness as a *substitute* for power—and this is nothing more than misogyny, disguised as feminist rhetoric. Being able to influence the gatekeepers is not the same as having your own key, but we've convinced ourselves that it is.

This is a broad claim to make, and so first I would like to clarify what I am *not* saying. First, I want to resist the possibility that my project be used to tell women (again) how to behave in the world, especially if it sounds like a repetition of the tired old refrain, "Cover up, or men will think you're easy." The Experiment was never about what men think—it's the opposite. In fact, I believe that the Suit is the costume for the primary role women are expected to play—that of a supporting cast member to men's lives and experiences—and I will reflect on how my taking off the Suit was the first step to getting off the stage. This book is not about men, except to the extent that the Suit supports toxic masculinity. And it does. This book is also not about what anyone other than me *should* do. It's simply an exploration of how beauty and empowerment have become conflated and how the religious traditions that inspire me view female modesty.

Second, modes of dress do not exist in a vacuum. There is always cultural context to consider, and so to advocate covering at all times would be meaningless and also potentially harmful. In ancient Rome, powerful women were veiled while slaves were forced to wear short skirts, signaling that their bodies belonged to others; in the 1920s, American women signaled their independence by wearing shorter and shorter skirts. In some parts of Africa, women go about their day with breasts bared and are not thought immodest; when Africans were dragged onto the auction block before the abolition of slavery, they were often stripped naked, a trauma meant to further dehumanize and objectify. In Afghanistan, the Taliban forced women to wear the burqa in public; in France, the niqab (a veil that covers the face except for the eyes, with a head scarf underneath) is banned, causing many Muslimahs (Muslim women) to mourn the loss of their option to cover. What is modest in some cultures is unnecessarily restrictive in others, and the significance of clothing choice changes with the context.

The culturally determined nature of the significance of clothing is precisely why covering, as opposed to exposure, was liberating for me, and it's a point I want to make here. Implying that my experiences of womanhood were normative was another criticism I received, and that one wasn't wrong. I was raised by a single dad, so I received an especially heaping dose of conflicting messages from the world around me about what my femininity was supposed to look like. My English-teacher-turned-writer father loudly decried pop culture and enforced a no-junk-food rule in the house, while my only-woman-in-her-practice-physician mom reveled in makeup, trashy TV, and ice cream.

And beyond the specificities of my own life, obviously every female is not a white, middle-class, cisgender (meaning that one's gender identity corresponds to their biological sex) North American. Women in Europe care a lot less about body hair than many American women do. Women of color have a different (compounded) set of adversities to contend with and issues to be managed when it comes to appearance, particularly the pressure to look lighter. Queer women may have yet another relationship to whether or not men find them attractive, but must also move through a world that grades women's worth by our adherence to male-centered beauty standards. Many cisgender women may feel imprisoned by what feel like cultural imperatives to wear heels and get plastic surgery, but for a transgender woman, these may be the keys to her long-overdue freedom. For me, a woman who internalized the idea that looking good and being liberated were the same thing, covering my body and avoiding makeup felt like rebellion.

Modern Western culture, however, interprets modesty in exactly the opposite way: for many of us in the West, a covered woman is an oppressed—or repressed—one. In ancient Rome where Christianity was born, for example, the veil was associated with marriage. Until recently, marriage meant male ownership of a woman. Not only her body—there was no such thing, legally speaking, as spousal rape in the US until the 1970s—but also her earnings, land, and property all belonged to the husband. If married women were literally owned by men, and only married women veiled, then it makes sense that we associate a covered woman with one who is not her own.

For much of American history, women who fought for liberation linked wearing less clothing with claiming more freedom. In 1850, the bloomer costume, which consisted of trousers and a loose blouse over a knee-length skirt, was defended by its feminist wearers, including Elizabeth Cady Stanton and Susan B. Anthony, with claims that it was not only healthier but also allowed women to move more freely and participate more fully in their own lives. Before bloomers, women wore tightly laced, disfiguring corsets with yards and yards of layered skirts, often with horsehair or straw sewn into the hems for weight, which were so long and voluminous that they scooped up trash and tobacco juice from the surfaces a woman walked upon.

Bloomers were abandoned quickly, however, amid cries that they represented "an affront to the God who had declared that each sex had certain attributes, certain spheres of action, and even distinct styles of dress."[1] Women were naturally subservient to men, it was said, and the Bloomer costume, in providing increased movement and public visibility, threatened that order. (Remember when I said that the Suit is a costume for women's roles as existing primarily in relation to men? This is *not* a new problem.)

In the sixties, during the second wave of feminism, short skirts were a way for women to express their refusal to be crammed into the demure-housewife box of the 1950s—more exposure, more freedom. During this time period, feminists also protested the 1968 Miss America pageant by discarding their bras into a Freedom Trash Can. (In fact, the bras were *not* burned. That never happened. It was a careless caption by a reporter that gave birth to the iconic bra-burning-feminist stereotype.[2]) From the 1850s to today, when we in the West think of women's liberation, many of us think of liberation from restrictive clothing.

But something has gone wrong—or maybe just too far—in the last twenty years or so. Beyoncé, the face of fierce feminism, has a body that is intimately familiar to us. From her video for "All the Single Ladies," one of the sexiest ever, in which she tells an ex she doesn't need him, to her performance in front of a giant lit-up "Feminist" sign while wearing what amounts to a bathing suit, Beyoncé routinely mingles empowerment and sex. When *Frozen*'s Queen Elsa, during her epic ballad "Let It Go," stops trying to deny her considerable talents, she suddenly decides that she must also be the only woman in her kingdom to wear a skintight dress with a slit up the front, shoulders bared, as she gazes up at everyone through her eyelashes. (Good thing the cold never bothered her anyway.) When comedians make fun of something, we know it's a cultural phenomenon, and Keegan-Michael Key as Mother Majesty, staring into a mirror in a dress, bald head shining, cackling, "Yes, girls. Being overly sexual and being strong is the same thing! *It's the same thing!*" is a great example: sexiness and power have supposedly become interchangeable.

Women's refusals to hide their bodies, by wearing bloomers or short skirts or not wearing bras, became an effective tool of empowerment because of the element of *choice*. Feminists have asserted, over and over, that liberated women show their bodies whenever they like, because the female body is not shameful. And that's true. But it's a message that has been repeated so often and so loudly that, almost without noticing, many women have come to *substitute* exposure for empowerment. More and more men try to persuade us to bare all, either on Snapchat or for *Girls Gone Wild*, by telling us not to be ashamed of our bodies. Little by little, *only* women who make themselves available for appraisal are liberated, and women who wear a hijab or who cover their hair after marriage are *always* oppressed. Little by little, feminist rhetoric is being used against women. Little by little, we have once again lost our choice.

Obviously, guys are not holding monthly meetings in smoky back rooms all over the country plotting to be sure that women continue to wear the Suit. The issue is cultural: everyone has helped create it, as women slut-shame—condemn another woman's style of dress or behavior as too sexual—and men tease by calling one another "pussy" or "sissy." Given this social environment, I wanted to explore alternative ways of moving through the world in a female body. The damaging effects of the West's cultural obsession with female youth and beauty are well known, but no one seems to know how to "do" empowerment without increasing exposure. I didn't anticipate the backlash against the project, but I should have: it proved my point. When I advocated modesty in the article for *Salon*, my loudest detractors were self-described feminist websites such as *Jezebel* and *XoJane*, and commenters of both genders alternately made fun of me for being "self-absorbed" and for advocating "oppressive gender norms." The truth was that the men were angry because I wasn't participating in their "right" to look at me; the women were angry because they thought I was caving to shame.

I understand the irony, of course, of trying to free myself from my obsession with beauty by changing my appearance. But I'm also not the only woman who experiences her choices for self-actualization this way. I know because when Hillary Rodham

Clinton was running for president, the most common dismissal tactic used was that she "looked old" or was "ugly," a criticism almost never used to discredit male politicians. I know, because lipstick ads promising "meaningful beauty" move units, instead of making us laugh with their ludicrous claim that a stick of chemicals can give women's lives meaning. I know because women are rushing to the plastic surgeon in the highest numbers in history with panic in their eyes: this is not mere vanity but terror that their age is rendering them invisible.[3] Kristin Scott Thomas, the gorgeous star of 1996's *The English Patient*, explained this phenomenon at fifty-three, saying, "When you're walking down the street, you get bumped into, people slam doors in your face—they just don't notice you."[4] That's scary, and it's nonsense.

Modesty is alluring for me because it represents an alternative way of being. It stands out against the backdrop of my culture, which tells me that to be relevant as a woman I have to be young, thin, white, and wear a certain costume. And really, in an age when women are bedazzling our vaginas after ripping out our pubic hair at the root, injecting toxins into our faces, implanting sacs of saltwater into our chests, and undergoing potentially life-threatening surgery to look thinner, how much further can women be expected to go in the pursuit of what is increasingly more Photoshop than female? For that matter, how much more psychological space would women have—not to mention hours in the day and money in the bank—if half our job in the world *wasn't* wearing the Suit? I discovered that during the Experiment, and let me tell you: it's not insignificant.

We in the United States have come a good way toward gender equality, and you'd think women should finally have control over our own bodies. But the fact that so many people felt totally comfortable telling me how to clothe my person indicates that American culture still has a long way to go. It speaks to the force of the pressure on women to expose. At the point during the Experiment when I felt most liberated, the thing that stunned me into temporary silence was the cultural slap in the face I received when I implied that maybe, just maybe, confusing hotness with power is just the same old bullshit dressed up to look like progress.

On the other hand, *can* covering the female body be disentangled from its history as a tool of shame, oppression, and victim blaming? Is it *possible*, at this point, for a woman to take off her makeup or not show her legs and not have it impact her negatively, either psychologically or out in the world? Or is more and more skin the only path left for those of us who want to be seen as strong? And if so, why does it feel like we're losing ground rather than gaining it? Discovering the answers to these questions was the aim of the Modesty Experiment and is the goal of this book.

Each chapter begins and ends with my experiences and inspirations for modesty. Because I was inspired by Jewish modesty in New York and Islamic modesty in seminary, I've chosen to explore covering through the lenses of the three Abrahamic religions: Islam, Christianity, and Judaism. All three have long histories of entwining misogyny and modesty, but none are devoid of alternative viewpoints on feminism and religion. In other words, it's the interpretation of the texts, not the texts themselves, that supports either progress (think of Dr. Martin Luther King Jr. and the way he brought Christianity to bear against racism) or the status quo (think of the hundreds of years of justification of racism by the church before that). Judaism, Christianity, and Islam all boast feminist scholarship; it's just that it doesn't get as much press as terrorists who stone women to death or priests who urge abused women to stay with their partners.

When I tell people about my nine months of modesty, they often ask me what I learned. I get the sense that what they want me to say—especially when it's a woman asking the question—is, "I learned that I'm beautiful on the inside, so what's on the outside doesn't matter!"

That is not what I fucking learned. At all.

I learned that the Suit is expensive and time-consuming and supports systemic racism but that wearing it makes a woman acceptable to the public. Alicia Keys took off her makeup after she was famous, and that's fantastic, but would she have gotten to where she is if she hadn't worn the Suit for all those auditions, concerts, and recording sessions earlier in her career? I can't say for certain, but I can say that as a young American woman, not wearing the Suit makes you invisible to a lot of people. Saying, "I learned that what matters is what's on the inside!" makes attention to the Suit an individual problem, as though high self-esteem is all that's needed to overcome its influence, and it's just not that simple. I hate that, but it's part of what the Experiment taught me.

I also learned that not all men *need* women to participate in this game. Because of how it's likely to be interpreted, I also hate to admit that I met my husband during the Experiment. He's been my biggest supporter while I wrote this book. And I learned that I can, in fact, go out in public without makeup and people won't shield their children's eyes. So that's good. Finally, I learned that I still like to look pretty, to tend to myself. Having good hair somehow makes me feel like I'm in control of my life.

But something is different now, and this has been the hardest thing to admit to myself, because I can't tie it up in a bow. I'm not sure what it is, but something crucial is missing from what I used to get out of the Suit, and its absence makes me feel bereft and a little lonely.

But I believe, with the interconnecting and horizon-broadening influence of technology, that it's time to move beyond the monolith of "If she won't bare all, it's because she's repressed." It's time for a world where women can just wear clothes and shoes and hairstyles that allow us to get on with our lives—you know, like dudes get to do, and have done, for centuries. It's interesting: the election of Donald Trump as president of the United States has pushed us in this direction just a tad. It means something that the most powerful elected man in the world is married to a woman whose claim to fame is how well she wears the Suit, and that he is known to have assaulted and violated women. There is proof now, whether one likes it or not, that the Suit does not empower women. It fact, it appears to do the opposite.

It's time for a world where the sexes are equal, instead of constantly pitting ludicrous abstractions about "real men" against "feminazis." It's time for women to be allowed to live our lives rather than being forced to constantly obsess over how we look. We can start by understanding what the Suit does to us, how it encourages us to see ourselves only as bit players for the men around us. Then we can start asking, as individuals, whether we really want to wear that costume anymore. We can start asking ourselves what would happen if women, as a gender, stopped accepting the Suit as a substitute for power and started demanding real equality.

I can tell you this: if you take off the Suit and say it's fun, people will be *super* mad.

I highly recommend it.

CHAPTER ONE

KATY PERRY IN A LEOPARD BUSTIER

The Problem with Sexy Feminism

MIDTOWN MANHATTAN, 2008

I am a member of an army: the Army of Coiffed Professionals.

I work on Fifth Avenue at a corporate ethics company, and one does not go to Midtown unless one is bringing the proverbial It—especially not if one works there. As the E train roars past the platform, I wonder how the women around me manage to keep their blowouts looking so good under the drying wool caps we wear. I wonder something similar in the summer, when the hot, stinky gusts that accompany each subway arrival blast our hair in a million different directions.

We sport a uniform: cinched waists, arms on display only if they are toned, high heels, tasteful makeup (never barefaced). The right shoes with the right belt, expensive and on trend, sexy but not slutty, somehow we all know the rules. It's probably just my imagination, but everyone else seems effortlessly comfortable in this getup. I am miserable, but I wear it because I have to. I find myself envying the Hasidic women in Brooklyn, who look stylish and comfortable in silk head scarves and long skirts.

In a small act of resistance, when the CEO isn't in the office, under my desk I wear a pair of slippers that look like sheep.

. . . . .

I was twenty-five, and it would be four years before I thought about modesty. Bursting onto the New York film scene and immediately getting hired as Christopher Nolan's go-to editor wasn't working out the way I had planned. The first film internship I had taken (unpaid, of course), thinking it would lead to employment in postproduction, turned out to be merely an office run on the free labor of an endless supply of starry-eyed kids. After about eight weeks of feeding the producer's cat and picking up cough medicine for her three-year-old, those stars would be thoroughly trampled on the sidewalks of the city and the kid would quit. On her way out the door, some twenty-two-year-old, fresh off the bus, would pop his head into the office and announce that he was here for his first day. And we interns wondered why the paid staff had no interest in networking with us. "What snobs," we'd say to each other. "When *I'm* head of post, I'll be nice to my interns."

Eventually I had to compromise and do whatever I could to stay in the city while I worked in film on the side. This led to the receptionist job, a position that I took because it paid the bills and, I thought, was probably not contributing to the downfall of American society (it was a corporate ethics firm, after all). During this time, I learned how good self-sufficiency was for my self-esteem.

Which led to my epic collapse when the recession hit in 2008 and I got laid off.

MEAT . . . MARKET? 2009
http://newyork.craigslist.org

Click: "gigs." Click: "talent."

"Party girls under thirty needed. Make extra money! $200–$400."

"Foot models needed. Strictly platonic, no nudity or sexual contact. $200/day."

Bursting into the New York job scene (again) and finding work as a receptionist, copy editor, housekeeper, tutor, runner, waitress, or cashier wasn't working out the way I'd planned. It seemed like everyone was suddenly jobless, and the market was flooded with desperate people looking for something, anything. Most of us—myself included—were not used to being unable to find work. I had two degrees; I had never thought of myself as someone who couldn't get a job, but here I was. After six months on unemployment, I was getting desperate.

"New York offers good unemployment benefits," I'd explained with strained cheerfulness to my brother when I returned to Tampa over Thanksgiving. "I have to take a bunch of vocational classes and prove that I'm always looking for work, but as long as I have that money—which is a third of what I used to make, standard New York state unemployment benefits—I can at least pay my rent."

He smirked at me over his beer. "Well, that's unfair," he said. "If they're helping you pay your bills, what reason do you have to look for work?" He snickered. "They're basically paying you to be lazy, aren't they?"

Click: "gigs." Click: "foot fetish party."

"Have your feet admired and worshiped by men while being very well paid for your time. Candidates must be sincere girl-next-door types and have flexible schedules. Include your photo and some background information about yourself."

I hesitated. *It looks creepy, but this isn't being exploited*, I told myself. *This is liberating. You're taking control of your body by using it to make money. You're a feminist.*

A week later in a freezing, incense-fragrant, tastefully decorated basement in the Meatpacking District, some dude is trying to persuade me, sotto voce, to give him a foot job through his pants. "I know you're new," he whispers, "but the other girls do it all the time. You just rub me through my pants with your feet. You don't even have to touch me."

No way, asshole, I think.

"I really can't," I say, trying to sound regretful. "You're only allowed to rub my feet or suck my toes. And you only have ten minutes." I could hear the voices of other couples behind the curtains. We were all in one big room, partitioned by cloth for privacy, and the lady who was running this "party" was very clear that if we engaged in activity that involved breasts or genitals, we could all go to jail for prostitution. The (first) Eliot Spitzer debacle was still fresh in New Yorkers' minds, so people were being careful. Ish.

The guy rolls his eyes. "A basement full of hot chicks, and I get the prude," he mutters. "Fine." What followed was the most resentful foot massage in history, for which I was paid twenty dollars. At the end of the night I'd made eighty dollars, which meant keeping my phone on, my lifeline to prospective jobs.

At one point, a young woman who called herself Ashley emerged, blond hair mussed, from behind one of the curtains where just before there had been a commotion. "What happened?" I whispered. The young man who'd been with her was smiling, but Ashley definitely was not. Apparently the guy had gotten handsy, kissing her and groping her. But instead of yelling or shoving him off her, Ashley just sat there—"I was a shot girl back home," she explained to me. "We had to let guys do shots out of our belly buttons and stuff. I'm used to guys being assholes." She was told never to come back.

On the subway home, I had a knot in my stomach. I felt like I had crossed some internal line. *If you were a stronger woman, you wouldn't be bothered by what just happened to you, and you'd do it again next week,* I told myself. *As long as you take responsibility for your safety and you don't let guys go too far like Ashley did, this is a way for you to take control of your life again.*

I couldn't sleep that night. I also never stopped berating myself for not being brave enough to go back.

OBJECT YOURSELF

It's a funny thing, the way a connection has been made for white women between self-objectification and a sense of personal power.

(Things are sometimes different for women of color, which will be discussed later in this chapter.) If you're truly empowered, says the narrative, you should sort of resemble one of the guys, especially when it comes to your views on the female body. Strong girls aren't bothered by porn depicting men doing things to women that many women would find painful, humiliating, or both in real life. In fact, we reenact these fantasies with our boyfriends, because that's just how cool we chicks are now. Women who are truly sex positive put their bodies on display—if you don't show skin, you must be ashamed of your femininity. We make porn too. Women who have good self-esteem aren't afraid to use their attractiveness to get what they want, especially if it means paying their bills, because not needing a man to take care of you is what feminism is all about. If you get a job because you're hot, good for you! If you're in a male-dominated field, you should be *glad* to be noticed for your body, because however you can get ahead is good enough. Strong womanhood means total comfort with being objectified, and if that bugs you, well, it's because you need to relax, baby.

This phenomenon even has a name. Ariel Levy, in her book *Female Chauvinist Pigs: Women and the Rise of Raunch Culture*, calls this cultural shift toward female self-objectification "the rise of the Female Chauvinist Pig." A female chauvinist pig, or "FCP" as Levy calls them, is a woman who claims her power by treating herself and other women the way women were treated back before the second wave of feminism in the 1960s. But because we're doing it to *ourselves*, claims the FCP, it's empowering. Levy likens the practice to "Tomming" (from the character in *Uncle Tom's Cabin*), a pejorative term used against a person, especially someone African American, who "deliberately upholds the stereotypes assigned to his or her marginalized group in the interest of getting ahead with the dominant group."[1] In other words, women who objectify themselves and other women, who say to men, "I don't like women. They're just so catty, you know?" and who champion all things macho while turning themselves into playthings for men—these are FCPs.

The biggest problem with this term, though it gives a name to and therefore opens dialogue about a phenomenon with deeply negative effects, is that it implies a malicious intent. "Female chauvinist pig" sounds like a woman who is a hypocrite at best and a misogynist at worst. While this may be true in some cases, not all women who dress up to go to work or take pole-dancing lessons are manipulative woman-haters with fabulous hair. Most of us self-objectify because we feel this is the only power afforded us: to be recognized in the wider culture as worthy of respect, we *must* wear the Beauty Suit, and how well we wear it is directly connected to how much access to power we have.

Men must appear put together and well groomed, of course, but they are not dressing for an amorphous woman the way that women, often subtly, are expected to do for men. Need an example? Turn on your TV: guys get funny commercials about mesh underpants that keep them cool, and women get shirtless models dancing to techno music while someone mumbles about the new You Should Be Thinner collection at Victoria's Secret. *My* underwear is supposed to make guys desire me; *guys'* underwear is supposed to let them get on with their lives.

Even little girls understand the relationship between self-objectification and power. A study in the journal *Sex Roles* explained that 72 percent of six- to seven-year-old girls chose a "sexy" doll (as opposed to a trendy but modestly dressed one) as most closely resembling both someone who was popular and their ideal self.[2] *Their ideal self.* Six-year-olds who aspire to be sexy are probably not FCPs. They're doing what kids do: measuring the world around them so they can gauge what they need to do to fit in and succeed. The parents who enter their five-year-olds in beauty pageants explain that "pageants build a child's confidence, give her a kind of poise that will someday be useful in job interviews and professional presentations."[3] In other words, learning how to perform female attractiveness, in the form of fake nails, spray tans, and blowing kisses at strangers, *teaches little girls how to succeed in the workforce.* Creepy, no? And not just for the children.

The world encourages self-objectification as a consequence of modern life: Facebook, Twitter, Instagram, even Pinterest and Etsy create platforms on which women and men curate our public selves. Soon, we can't see ourselves as anything other than these hashtagged, shared, and liked people we've created. Between a woman's online persona, being expected to *look* desirable but not *experience* desire (see every bit of research on teenage girls for the last ten years), and the Suit, no wonder millions of women are wandering around with flawless exteriors who don't even know they *have* an interior, much less who that person is.

SKIN = LIBERATION

In pop culture for at least the last twenty years, sex appeal and strength have become increasingly indistinguishable. Lara Croft, protagonist of the *Tomb Raider* video game, kicks ass in impractically tight, impractically short pants; the curves on her rear prominently featured as she kills bad guys. Zoe Saldana is a capable heroine from the *Guardians of the Galaxy* franchise whose cleavage is also highlighted in her frequent fistfights. Katniss Everdeen, protagonist of *The Hunger Games*, fares better in the movie version of the story, with less impractical costuming and motivations that seem to come from a desire to stand up for herself and her community, rather than to help a male hero accomplish his goals. Of course, Jennifer Lawrence, the actor playing Katniss, was reminded of her place as male property in what became known as Celebgate, when Redditors gloated upon the leakage of nude selfies with lascivious statements about how delightfully powerless Lawrence was to decide who was allowed to see her body. "In the real world, a girl like you would never give me the time of day," one Redditor gleefully wrote. "BUT IT AIN'T UP TO YOU NOW, IS IT BITCH?!"

In the music industry, female empowerment anthems are usually paired with the sexual objectification of the singer. In the video for Katy Perry's "Roar," Perry crash-lands in a jungle with a selfie-taking, duckface-pulling man, presumably her boyfriend.

Her clothing is that of a stereotypical "repressed" librarian: a long-sleeved, high-collared blouse, a pencil skirt, and a scarf covering her chest. She spends the video liberating herself from her lame boyfriend (actually, outside circumstances liberate her *from* him—he gets taken out by a tiger) and finding her strength, and as she does so, her costume gets skimpier. In the triumphant final chorus, Perry sits on a throne with her legs open in a leopard-print bustier and a grass skirt, palm fronds covering her crotch, and paints her lips bright red with berries she has found.

Study after study has proven that people respond to nonverbal cues far more readily than verbal ones, and no matter what pop feminist icons say, as long as women are still expected to make men drool before they make their case, things are going to stay exactly as they are. "Born This Way," a self-acceptance anthem, shows us a glistening, wiry Lady Gaga, who herself has struggled with eating disorders, writhing in a bikini. (One wonders about the challenge of a twenty-five-year-old white woman accepting herself with an army of diet coaches, personal trainers, and stylists at hand.) Rapper Iggy Azalea, while riding a bike in skintight leggings, tells us how hard she's had to "Work" to provide for herself, as the camera repeatedly pans down to show us her butt.

One might argue that Gaga and Iggy (and, often, Beyoncé) are singing about empowerment or kicking ass while putting their bodies on display because "sex sells," not because strength and hotness are developing a close relationship. But the issue with this argument is obvious: female sex sells to straight guys and possibly queer women (who are also, just to complicate things, objectified). What about what the other at-least-half of the population—straight women, gay men, and anyone who isn't turned on by the constant onslaught of glistening thighs and parted, lacquered lips—wants to see? Also interesting to note is that one of the most common ways to discredit (that is, not just insult but also invalidate) a woman is to call her ugly. Countless Tumblr posts describe guys on Tinder who have been rejected by women and then tell them they are "not hot enough to be acting like this" and that they are "stuck-up bitches" for politely refusing gallant offers to "put my meat in your mouth." (This was an actual conversation.) As though beauty and the right to respect are directly proportional.

By contrast, Sheryl Sandberg appeared on the March 2013 cover of *Time*, with the caption "Her mission to reboot feminism." Wearing a tasteful but still sexy ensemble—red and fitted to show her tiny waist, with a V-neck, a pencil skirt, and the requisite powerful-woman heels—Sandberg is pictured in a full-body shot. In contrast, Chris Christie's, Marco Rubio's, and Barack Obama's covers featured close-ups of their faces. *Time*'s audience seems to need to see that the new face of feminism is also very attractive. Why is it so important that this new paradigm of empowerment is sexy? Because in this so-called postfeminist world, where women post pictures of themselves online with signs completing the phrase "I don't need feminism because…" a woman is embraced by the wider culture as worth listening to only if she shows a little skin, and looks good doing it.

THE COMMON DENOMINATOR: WEAPONIZED SHAME

Men are not the only ones supporting this connection between sex appeal and feminist empowerment. Men who want to see lots of flesh benefit from the collective cries to "Take it off," as shorthand for "Free yourself," but male desire alone isn't enough to perpetuate it. What keeps women grabbing for the brass ring of power through sex appeal is that for too long female sexuality was associated with shame. And when our feminist foremothers claimed a woman's right to control her own body, they often expressed their newfound liberation by wearing clothes deemed offensive or inappropriate by the wider culture (like the aforementioned bloomers). In general, when one thinks of feminist movements, one thinks of women giving the establishment the finger by refusing to cave to respectability politics.

Perhaps this is why so many feminist women believe that wearing fishnets or a bustier is another rebellion; "sexy as strong" isn't necessarily a feminist betrayal. Some of us, when we wear six-inch stilettos, are rejecting the notion that if a woman dresses provocatively she should be devalued or mocked. For some, dressing provocatively is a way of standing up against the narrative that women who dress a certain way are "asking for it."

It's also true that attractive people of both sexes are statistically more likely to be successful, earning 3 to 4 percent more than their less-attractive counterparts. However, only women must deal with the practice of "slut shaming." Look at the comments section on any online article about or by a woman, especially if she has been sexually victimized, and you will see that slut shaming through threats, bullying, and derision is a favored weapon to silence.

Slut shaming isn't always couched in abusive language or insults. Sometimes it takes the form of so-called considered arguments that if a woman doesn't want to be violated, she shouldn't make it so easy to be victimized. For example, in the Celebgate nude-photo leaks of Jennifer Lawrence and other celebrities, thousands of private nude selfies were leaked onto the internet—and the public response was to tell the wronged women that hey, maybe if they didn't want those pictures in cyberspace, they shouldn't have taken them in the first place. This is the argument that continues to be used every time there's a news story about a young woman being bullied via the dissemination of her nudes by an ex-boyfriend or even about child-pornography rings based on the sale of these pictures to third parties by recipients. Slut shaming goes hand in hand with victim blaming, which tries to make rape and assault victims seem responsible for their attacks.

And again, the problem of slut shaming is not men foisting their views upon women; it's a cultural phenomenon, and as participants in American culture, women slut-shame too. When a sixteen-year-old girl in Steubenville, Ohio, was raped while other students filmed it (and then spread the videos and pictures via Facebook and Twitter), Serena Williams was quoted in *Rolling Stone* as saying, "She's sixteen, why was she that drunk where she doesn't remember? It could have been much worse. She's lucky.

Obviously, I don't know, maybe she wasn't a virgin, but she shouldn't have put herself in that position, unless they slipped her something, then that's different."[4] No, that's slut shaming ("She shouldn't have put herself in that position") and victim blaming ("She's sixteen, why was she that drunk where she doesn't remember? It could have been much worse. She's lucky."). And what the hell does her being a virgin have to do with anything, Strong Liberated Role Model Serena? Williams later apologized, but the damage was done.

This is still how people talk about what happens when men behave like sinister toddlers who have decided they have a right to take what they want: it's the woman's fault. Women must have some serious magical powers we're unfamiliar with to force men to commit inhuman acts. Too bad women can't use our irresistible influence to get equal pay.

SEXY FEMINISM

In their 2013 book *Sexy Feminism: A Girl's Guide to Love, Success, and Style*, Jennifer Keishin Armstrong and Heather Wood Rudúlph set out to "detonate, once and for all, those pervasive myths about feminism. You know, that it wrecks homes and happiness, that it hates men and sex and anything pretty, and that it's a general drag."[5] Armstrong and Rudúlph attempt to navigate the labyrinthine discussions about modern feminism, which is to say they try to explain what being a feminist means without invalidating anyone's life choices. This is quite an undertaking: especially with the advent of the internet, it seems that any choice a woman makes nowadays is subject to public condemnation, and Armstrong and Rudúlph devote great time and care to dissecting the forces that contribute to the difficulty of being female in modern Western culture.

The crux of the *Sexy Feminism* argument is a hallmark of what some are calling fourth-wave feminism (first wave: getting the right to vote; second wave: the 1960s and not-bra-burning protesters; third wave: revolutionary authors Rebecca Walker, who introduced the concept of the oppression of the female voice in American culture, and Naomi Wolf, who pointed out the abusive inconsistencies about our bodies that are used to control women). The most important feature of fourth-wave feminism, say Armstrong and Rudúlph, is that of individual choice. Prescriptive notions of what a feminist woman looks like are not only useless—every woman's life experience is different—but also potentially harmful, and the point of *Sexy Feminism* is that each woman has a right to heed her inner voice and make choices that are in alignment with what her heart says, and that no one, least of all other women, should be telling another woman she's living her own life wrong.

For example, Armstrong and Rudúlph have a chapter called "Vanity Is Not a Feminist Sin." Yes! Erin La Rosa, a *BuzzFeed* staff writer, went makeup-free for a week, and the response almost broke the internet (take that, Kim Kardashian). According to *BuzzFeed*, the article got almost three million hits, and as of this writing, there are almost one thousand comments. The discussion is impassioned: Are women who wear makeup vain? Is it really that impressive for a thirtyish, clear-skinned, beautiful woman to eschew makeup for a week? In many comments, there seems to be an undercurrent of "If women really loved themselves, they wouldn't need makeup!" But can a woman love herself and wear makeup? Of course, say Armstrong and Rudúlph: as long as she is expressing herself, and she's done her homework about which brands are sufficiently feminist (Bobbi Brown, Tarte, and MAC are some examples they give—interesting that these brands are also rather expensive), she can wear whatever she wants on her face. Also, say the Sexy Feminists, don't judge: "If one of your coworkers rocks bleached-blond hair, blue eyeshadow, and frosted pink lip gloss, let the woman have her look. If she feels good in her own skin, what do you care? Her individuality is beautiful."[6]

The same choice-championing arguments apply to *weight loss* (sensible eating and exercise are feminist because they're about self-care; self-punishing diets are not), *plastic surgery* (unless you identify as trans and your true self really is expressed by a different body, in most cases plastic surgery is not a feminist act because it's about "fixing" your already fine self), *fashion* (fashion as self-expression is empowering; wearing restrictive clothing to keep your "over-bearing boyfriend" happy, not so much), and *sex* (if you truly like it, there's nothing off-limits, but don't do anything that makes you uncomfortable). So Sexy Feminism is about two things, really: heeding your voice, and having a choice. Being an empowered woman means living authentically through a combination of self-reflection, media savvy, and careful consumerism. If this means the rejection of slut shaming by wearing short skirts, great—as long as that choice is authentically yours.

So what's the problem with all this voice-choice feminism? Don't women have all the power we want to listen to our hearts and choose to wear makeup or not, to get plastic surgery or diet, to have crazy threesomes or stay celibate? Of course, but much of *Sexy Feminism*, though well-intentioned and certainly positive, centers mostly on one thing: women's bodies. More than half the chapters are about our physical selves, whether that's fashion as empowerment or the recent trend of bedazzling our vaginas. This isn't necessarily off the mark, considering that almost all the messages women receive are about our bodies and what to do with them, whom to show them to, and how. We do need someone to tell us that yes, Virginia, we can do what we want with our physical selves. However, it's troubling just how much of being a feminist woman still focuses on how we look. It seems suspiciously like FCP-ism. This may be simply a response to the world we live in, but still.

Another problematic element of defining "being a feminist" as following one's inner voice is that we don't live in a world where it's at all easy for most girls and women to do that. I've said before that women are culturally expected to be bit players in men's lives. What I mean is that we're made to be responsible for the physical and psychological comfort of the men around us. This is not just being compassionate or kind to the people we love; that is basic humanity. No, this is emotional custodianship of every man we meet, altering our behavior so that *all* the men in our lives—partners, yoga instructors, coworkers, even strangers on the street—have to endure a minimum of discomfort.

It's evident when we speak haltingly to a boss so that he sees us as a team player when it comes time for performance reviews; it's evident when the guy at the grocery store winks at us and we respond with a shy smile so he doesn't follow us out to the parking lot hurling obscenities; it's evident when we couch our criticisms of male employees with flattery and praise so that they never feel "attacked" and lodge a complaint against us. The less secure a man is, the harder women must work to keep from experiencing negative consequences when we deal with him. Even if we grow up with fantastic fathers and kind brothers, we must still know how to protect men's egos, *especially* if they are attracted to us.

What this means is that as young girls, we learn to ignore our own inner voices in favor of hearing what men need from us. This is not a matter of low self-esteem; it's just survival. The ability to manipulate men so they do not hurt us becomes instinctive very early on, and many women are not aware that we even have an inner voice, much less how to heed it, until later in life.

Also, no matter what choices women make, being female seems to come with a sign that says, "Please feel free to comment on what you think I should be doing, wearing, and saying! Don't hold back. You don't have to know me to know what's good for me." The internet is a big purveyor of this pressure; users feel they have a right to tell women what to do. And the days when male preachers devoted entire Sundays to sermons on the dress and behavior of the ideal Christian woman are hardly ancient history. Further, as Peggy Orenstein explored in her 2011 work *Cinderella Ate My Daughter: Dispatches from the Front Lines of the New Girlie-Girl Culture*, the option we supposedly have now to look hot while we do everything men do is not as freely undertaken as we'd like to think. The line between coercion and choice gets blurry when girls grow up in a culture that steeps us in pink Disney princesses and the teen-girl icon of the moment and then socially punishes us when we do not conform. In fact, says Orenstein, instead of having more choice, women and girls are "straddling a contradiction: struggling to fulfill all the new expectations we have for them without letting go of the old ones.... They now feel they must not only 'have it all,' but be it all: Cinderella *and* Supergirl. Aggressive *and* agreeable. Smart *and* stunning."[7] Sound familiar?

Maybe not everyone is like me, and they're self-directed enough not to be bothered by the constant pressure exerted by the world for women to look twenty-one until we die. But Armstrong and Rudúlph include their backgrounds in the beginning of *Sexy Feminism*, and while I'm sure their lives were not perfect, they both grew up in white, middle-class homes with parents who encouraged them to be themselves. Both had parents (who were together) who had the time and the income to be at home most of the time; Armstrong's parents were both aware of gender dynamics and filled her with a sense that she deserved to be treated as equal to men by the world. Rudúlph's parents were "tree-hugging flower children" who were into "eschewing materialism, embracing unity, and streamlining your life."[8] Her parents pushed their kids "to be self-sufficient and accountable."[9]

Both authors recognize their privilege, of course, but the fact remains: most of us do not grow up with what these women did. Parents who have the time, education, and interest to talk to their kids about things like gender roles while staying home with them to grow their own food are rare, especially in underprivileged communities. It is hard, if not impossible, to hear your authentic voice when you are constantly battling racism, poverty, violence, poor education, and any of the myriad other issues associated with not growing up in a white, middle-class family.

Even for many women who were blessed with the "right" skin color, neighborhood, and school, being silenced and having our perceptions devalued is how we grew up. If you were one of the millions of Americans raised by a parent with a substance abuse problem, molding yourself to what the user needed you to be became the way to survive. If you had a family member who was one of the "tens of millions" (according to the National Institute of Mental Health) of people who struggle with mental illness—or if you're one yourself—you know how reality distorting that can be, and how quickly one's own perceptions get twisted and buried.

Yes, being human means some measure of suffering, and we're all silenced or restrained in one way or another. But given all these factors, how likely is it that the rush women get when we feel desired by strangers comes from our own concept of what empowerment feels like to us? Far more likely is that the implicit approval we obtain when someone checks us out simply feels like a drink of water in an endless desert of "Your waist is too thick. Your skin isn't light enough. Your calves aren't toned. Your hair isn't long enough, and also you're too hairy. Your clothes are out of date. *And look out, here comes thirty!*"

To be a truly informed, well-rounded Sexy Feminist, you need to hear and heed your inner voice, which is the only thing that makes wearing high heels and getting Brazilian waxes truly feminist choices. If we lived in a world where self-value was the norm for all women, *and not wearing the Beauty Suit didn't impact us negatively*, then we really could be Sexy Feminists. As it is, I just don't think most of us have any idea where to begin.

#NOTALLWOMEN

Years before I moved to New York, I lived in the world's tiniest, ugliest studio apartment in Tallahassee. It just so happened that my friend Nicole, a smart, funny African American woman with whom I'd gone to film school and with whom I have never really gotten to spend enough time, was willing to help me paint it to look less gulag-y.

I had decided to do two walls in purple and two in green, and Nicole took the green walls. I can't remember how we got on the topic, but somehow we ended up talking about sexism in the film industry. At one point I had a revelation. I looked up at Nicole on her ladder, my eyes wide with wonder at my own brilliance. "Hey,"

I said, "African American women's experience is different from white women's, isn't it?"

That she did not dump paint on my head is a testament to Nicole's character. Instead she turned to me, nodding earnestly. "Yes," she said. "Yes, it is."

Looking back on this moment in my life, I am grateful that I had a friend who was kind enough not to roll her eyes and say, "You're twenty-three years old, and you're *just now* realizing this?" Which she could have. She could also have said, "Yep," and then closed the discussion, because she had probably had this very same talk with countless white people in her life. Now, more than ten years later, most people of color I know do not want to talk to white folks about what it's like to be black and brown in America, largely because they're tired of educating us on what we can find out for ourselves if we just look for the information. And as I found when I conceived of the Modesty Experiment, women of color have a different relationship to modesty and liberation than do white women.

In African American communities, the equation of sexiness equals power often breaks down. For black women who come from a history of enforced nudity on the auction block and rape at the hands of white slave owners, the right to dictate who sees how much of one's body is often associated with power and personhood. Patricia, a twentysomething black pastor in Ohio, explained, "In a context where people can strip you down without your consent, being able to choose whether to stay covered or not covered is a blessing. And liberating." Many black women are taught by their mothers and grandmothers that looking one's best, but not looking too sexual, is a sign of respect for others and oneself.

This standard is most visible in the church, where one is expected to look one's best for God, but it's not exclusive to church communities. According to Ella, a sixtysomething former schoolteacher, now a pastor in Mississippi, covering "was a part of African American culture as a whole. I have several African outfits from when I went to Zimbabwe [for a semester in seminary]. Every gift I received was cloth. It was like, 'We have to make sure you have something to wear.' Not only was it cloth, but people actually paid for me to have my dresses made. And they were always long, and never too low cut. I think it comes from the African culture itself that was brought into this country. And we've evolved, of course. But I think it started there." Even a black woman with a head scarf is not an uncommon sight.

Modest dress is not universal among black women, of course, and in fact, it's becoming less common. Both Patricia and Ella indicated that the older generations were more invested in covering than today's youth. Ella told me, "I don't believe the younger people think about [modesty]. It's not taught anymore. It was taught for us." This may be because younger generations often do things that their elders consider too permissive. Nonetheless, from head wraps to long dresses, modesty as power is not as foreign a concept for African American women as it is for white women.

Even though African American women may feel more comfortable exposing their bodies today, they still do not have the option of using beauty as power, simply because beauty standards are still very, very white. Black women, though more visible in pop culture of late, thanks in large part to women such as the prolific producer, director, and author Shonda Rhimes and writer-director Ava DuVernay, are still not generally portrayed as desirable or sexy unless they emulate whiteness, by lightening their skin or straightening their hair. They may be strong, loud, or outspoken, but in a world where passivity and sexual submission are equated with femininity, these adjectives are hardly compliments. In fact, they're merely repetitions of the idea that black women are "scary" and therefore undesirable, worthy of condemnation and devaluation. Black features on white women are OK—Kim Kardashian's appropriation of racist propaganda in *Paper* magazine's Break the Internet project, in which she reenacted an old photo of Grace Jones from a book called *Jungle Fever*, received plenty of positive attention—but black features on actual black women are alternately fetishized and derided. If black female sexuality makes an appearance, it is portrayed as over the top and needing to be tamed, like Nicki Minaj's butt-baring "Anaconda" single cover—not like pleasingly submissive white women.

Latina, Hispanic, and Chicana (of Mexican heritage) women, although they are not racially considered white, are usually portrayed in heavily sexualized ways on TV and in movies. They are sexy *because* they are different, but they can conform to white standards of beauty more easily than black women. This is a good example of the dubiousness of hot as strong: their power supposedly comes not from being a whole person with a different ethnic origin but from being "exotic" (code for "nonwhite but still sexy"). The "fiery Latina," which the actors Sofia Vergara and Eva Longoria typify, is outspoken, yes, but she is also pale enough (with straight enough hair) to satisfy the requirements of feminine desirability. She may speak her mind, but she still wears the Suit.

However, many Latina women are explicitly aware, in a way white women often are not, that beauty is not an absolute value and that it is racially weighted. Professor in the Department of Chicana/o Studies at the University of California at Santa Barbara, Aída Hurtado surveyed 101 of her Chicana students. "Many respondents," she says, "expressed the view that beauty was socially constructed and extremely subjective. They knew that women's energies were distracted from other endeavors because society rewards women for their physical appearance."[10] In the mostly white suburb where I grew up, an idea like that sounds like radical feminist propaganda.

This is not to say Latina and Chicana women are somehow beyond the influence of beauty culture. In fact, writes half–Puerto Rican author Alida Nugent of her own relationship with her appearance, "a lot of the time things like 'putting time into your appearance' can be thought of as vapid and vain. I never felt that way. I felt too scared at what would happen if I didn't."[11] However, many Latina, Hispanic, and Chicana women engage more critically with the Suit than white women do. Further, explains Hurtado, many of the respondents in her study had family members who encouraged them to see themselves as beautiful in the way of

indigenous women, rather than comparing them to white standards of beauty. Again, in my mostly white suburb, mothers were
more likely to tell their daughters to lose weight or wear makeup
than to tell them not to worry too much about mainstream beauty
expectations.

East Asian women are also often highly fetishized, and in
downright disturbing ways that betray American culture's persistent association between feminine desirability and a lack of agency.
Chinese, Japanese, and Korean women are perceived as particularly
sexy because they are believed to innately personify antiquated notions of feminine perfection: white, thin, domestically gifted, and,
above all, eager to please men. Rachel, an Asian actor in New York
City, shocked me when she told me that she is catcalled literally
every single day by men muttering "Konnichiwa" ("Hello") and
"Ooh, Asian persuasion" as they pass her. Rachel explained that
Asian women are seen as arm candy precisely because they are perceived to be "submissive, polite, clean, and docile."

This American Life producer Stephanie Foo explains a horrifying, but common, phenomenon in an episode of the podcast *Reply
All* in which Foo realizes that her boyfriend dates only Asian
women.[12] Rachel readily confirmed that this happens to "every
Asian woman I know. You have to ask what his [the potential
mate's] exes look like, because he might have—this is a bad term,
but it's what they call it—'Yellow Fever.'" To have an Asian girlfriend is to have the Hottest Girlfriend, because she hasn't been
contaminated by that pesky independence thing. Most white
women give no sympathy to creeped-out Asian women, though.
To be idealized is to be valued. Essentially, as long as a woman is
pale enough to uphold white standards of beauty, she is deemed
worthy of objectification.

Looking at the Suit from the perspectives of women of color
reveals two kinds of power: the kind that comes from fulfilling the
dominant culture's ideals and the kind that comes from bucking
those ideals and seeing oneself as a whole person. The first, as Nugent says, "feels like a passive thing, a handing over of power rather

than one we can harness"; the second is true strength.[13] It still feels good, in other words, to get dolled up, because I get a charge out of being pretty enough to be looked at; but getting my power from a flatiron means I may not even realize that I need the other kind of strength far more. (It also makes me much more boring.)

Hotness as power has a heavily racist component that white women do not consider simply because we do not have to. If female worth is measured by beauty, and beauty is measured by pallor, then the whiter a woman is, the more value she has. This means that white women benefit from beauty standards that centralize us as the ideal, so we fight to maintain them. In fact, this whole project has much to do with my race: I don't think there would've been a *Salon* article about a black woman covering her hair and not wearing makeup, but when a white woman publicly deprives men of the ability to look at her, everyone has an opinion about it.

Also, whether white women admit it to ourselves or not, our privilege is costing us something. Although we know our ability to fit into the Suit gives us some measure of visibility, deep down, we know that it's not real power we're getting. A lifetime of dieting and plastic surgery, worrying about wrinkles and whether our hair color washes us out, takes its toll, especially because the older we get, the more surely we know just how much time and money we've wasted worrying about the Suit. By the time we're forty, we may feel the sacrifice just wasn't worth it, and for some of us, bitterness is creeping in. But because our worth depends on our desirability and the ideal woman does not get angry, we have nothing to do with all our resentment and rage.

As a result, we fight viciously over what little turf we do have. When black women try to discuss racism with white women, we accuse them of taking attention away from the real issues. We call them too angry, or we tell them they just need to get over it. Because we've never felt heard or validated, we refuse to listen or validate, and white feminist women like me are particularly guilty of this. There's only so much room at the top in a culture where one demographic has most of the power, and the Suit keeps white women competing for it rather than realizing the whole system is broken.

Open acknowledgment that the wider culture does not have their best interests at heart is one way in which people of color have responded to the demands of living in a world that tells them they have no worth because they are not white. Perhaps white women also need to stop accepting the crumbs of so-called empowerment offered when we adhere to what the dominant culture says we should be. The oppression of sexism and the oppression of racism are not comparable, but perhaps white women can also learn to acknowledge that the world we live in is not ours. Or at least it was not built by us, and it is not *for* us.

NOT OUR WORLD: TOXIC MASCULINITY

I feel it necessary to explain at this point that, contrary to what a relative once accused me of on Facebook, I am not a man-hater. I do not believe that most men consciously—*consciously*—wish ill upon women. However, Western culture is one in which men's desires and comfort take priority over those of women, even when women's safety, health, or sanity is threatened. And when this order is upset, many men tend to get angry, because who, honestly, *wouldn't* want to live in a world where they could expect their desires to be catered to, simply because they exist? (It's like Disneyland, only you never have to leave!) The world men live in is not our world, and it is actively dangerous for us. Let me bring in some case studies to show you what I mean.

From what time I've been able to stomach spending in online men's rights forums, many men believe, consciously or unconsciously, that maleness entitles one to sex with whatever woman they choose. According to Rebecca Solnit, many attacks against women begin with the rejection of an advance from a man, whether he is her partner or a stranger on the street.[14] This reminds us of the supporting role every woman must learn as soon as possible: we must protect men's egos if they express interest; if we do not, much of the time they will hurt us, physically or otherwise. Further supporting the ownership paradigm, the murder of a woman by her former partner is often instigated by her leaving him (or trying to).

Another strain of reasoning that I've seen among men's rights activists is that their attraction to us makes women automatically responsible for reciprocating favorably, an attitude that also shows up, albeit more subtly, among less radical men. This attitude does not always play out in violent ways; witness complaints about the Friend Zone, in which men who want sex with a woman get angry and bitter when they are "reduced" to "mere" friendship with her. Not all men believe this, but it is what they are taught. It does not matter if an individual man is not, and has never been, violent; all men benefit from those who punish women for refusing to play the roles asked of them.

In an extreme example of male entitlement, in 2014, Elliot Rodger killed six people near the University of California, Santa Barbara, with the justification that if women had slept with him, then he wouldn't have turned out to be a monster. Somehow, in media coverage and the public eye, Rodger became perceived as a mentally ill outlier instead of what he was: a poster boy for what Katie McDonough, in her *Salon* article, called "toxic masculinity." To be clear, Rodger was certainly called a killer, but the public's resistance to connecting his murderous spree with misogyny—*misogyny he enumerated in the video he made before killing all those people*—was overwhelming. In the comments sections of the articles and videos about the whole awful episode, thousands of women expressed familiarity with this kind of thinking: the entitlement, the rage, the self-aggrandizing violence. In return, thousands of men told those women they were being hysterical.

Solnit also tells us that the leading cause of death among pregnant women is violence inflicted by their spouses. Let me say that again: *if a pregnant woman dies, it is most likely to be because her spouse killed her.* The *New York Times* op-ed columnist Nicolas Kristof writes, "Women worldwide ages fifteen through forty-four are more likely to die or be maimed because of male violence than because of cancer, malaria, war and traffic accidents combined."[15] Given all the pink ribbons and marches, all the advice to wear a seatbelt and use hand sanitizer, I would think that I should be most afraid of lumps in my breasts and drunk drivers. As it turns out, if I do not die of old age, I am most likely to be beaten to death or shot, most likely by someone who tells me he loves—or at least desires—me.

Every woman I know has at least one personal story of being stalked or knows another woman who has had a stalker. When we call the police, we're ignored—until the woman turns up dead, at which point the outcry of "Why wasn't something done sooner?" goes up, then dies, having been drowned out in an avalanche of similar stories. Cases like that of Jasmine Wright, who was killed by a maintenance man in her building who had a record of attempted rape and was still hired for a job that granted him access to women's homes, are so common that hardly anyone notices them anymore.

Male ownership of female bodies is not just about sex. Rhetoric against female reproductive rights not only causes gun violence, as in the case of Robert Lewis Dear at a Planned Parenthood clinic in Colorado ("I am a warrior for the babies," he insisted at a hearing on December 23, 2015), but also spurs repeated government shutdowns, endless legal maneuvering, and prohibitive rules that result in male control over women's bodies being codified into law. More than 50 percent of guests on political talk shows, from CNN to Fox News, are white men, meaning that more than half of the so-called experts on everything from racism to reproductive rights are people who are not directly affected by either of those issues. From 2010 to 2013, more than 70 percent of TV-show directors were white men, meaning again that white guys control most of the portrayals of other races and genders you see when you turn on the TV at night.[16] The demographics of those in power, both culturally and politically, are so overwhelmingly skewed in favor of European American men that it's amazing anyone would argue for the existence of equal representation at all, much less assert that white maleness is under attack. This isn't a conspiracy; it's the reality of the world in which all of us live.

The internet hasn't proven to be the egalitarian sphere many were hoping for either. Look at the trolls on Reddit and Twitter, who are famous for punishing outspoken women via doxxing (revealing a woman's private details, such as her home address or the names of her children) or rape threats. In the case of the feminist author Lindy West, one young man created a fake Twitter account with her dead father's name in order to abuse her. Another good example is GamerGate, a fracas in which female gamers and feminists were threatened and harassed for their attempts to take male online gamers to task for the blatantly misogynistic world of online gaming. *Mother Jones* reports that "closing the so-called digital divide still leaves a noticeable gap; the more privileged your background, the more likely that you'll reap the additional benefits of new technologies."[17]

In other words, the advent of the internet has reinforced cultural divides instead of helping us learn to talk to one another. Again: look at the comments section for any article, from science to politics. The needlessly contentious debates are so asinine that many websites, such as *Slate* and *Popular Science*, have eliminated their comments sections altogether. According to *Popular Science*'s article "Why We're Shutting Off Our Comments": "Commenters shape public opinion; public opinion shapes public policy; public policy shapes how and whether and what research gets funded— you start to see why we feel compelled to hit the 'off' switch."[18] And have you read anything on feminism online, at all, ever? Prepare to have your eyebrows burned off by the collective outrage of thousands of men who are "being discriminated against."

So, to recap: our husbands are statistically the most likely to kill us, the internet responds with death threats to every woman with an opinion, and men continue to assert their victimhood at the hands of women who will not sleep with them. But it's cool, because sometimes when we have a lot of time and money we can *make* guys want to have sex with us.

This is not our world, it is not a culture made to benefit us, and to tell us that we're empowered because we can wear whatever we want insults our intelligence and erodes our self-esteem. Enough is enough.

USING THE SYSTEM AGAINST ITSELF

As someone who loves makeup and doing my hair, I can say that looking good *can* feel empowering. And I have no right to tell anyone what to do, especially since my aim is not to silence women but to give us a way to talk about what it feels like to live in a culture that objectifies us, and then has the gall to tell us that being fuckable and being respected are the same thing. But it's a dangerous thing to use a corrupt system against itself, even if *you* know your goal is sabotage.

For many women, donning the Beauty Suit day after day is teaching us something dangerous. When we feel that we must wear a costume to be validated or even visible, we are paradoxically practicing a phenomenon called self-concealment. According to the *Journal of Social and Clinical Psychology*, self-concealment is "the active concealment from others of personal information that one perceives as negative or distressing," and it refers to everything from lying about one's own preferences to self-objectification.[19] We smile when we're angry and channel our loneliness into shopping in the name of self-concealment; we also wear Spanx, color our hair, and use, on average, seventeen appearance-altering products on our bodies every day.

Self-concealment in the name of beauty may seem like merely a physical conceit, but it's not. It's a habit that works its way in, from our skin to our souls. Our internal voices, the ones that might allow us to choose whether to self-objectify as a feminist statement or to cover our thighs because we feel better that way, become quieter and quieter. According to the same study, self-concealment directly correlates with depression, anxiety, and an inability to form healthy relationships and boundaries. The more we hide, the smaller we become.

Like snowflakes, moments of self-concealment to which the Beauty Suit has inured us fall, gradually blanketing us in cold and silence. We dance on bars because our sex appeal is "liberating," ignoring the little voice in our head that says we feel exposed. We let our partner do things to us in bed we're not really OK with, but because we're so used to playing a secondary role in our own life, we turn down the volume on our fear and discomfort. We show our creepy supervisor patience when he just won't leave us alone, because if we wound his ego there will be consequences. When we're groped on the bus, instead of whipping around and confronting the guy, we pretend it didn't happen, then get doubly punished when our husband is angry at us for our response. We become so used to self-silencing that soon the *only* surefire way we know to feel powerful is to look flawless. And this serves the system just fine—the system where you have to wear a Suit that defuses your threat to white male cultural dominance just to leave the house, and then pretend it's a sufficient substitute for that little voice you can no longer hear.

ALMOST: CHELSEA, EARLY 2009

"I told you not to get off there," says the buzzing voice of the woman in my ear. "I gave you specific directions."

I look around for street signs. Chelsea is oddly deserted at night compared to the rest of the city, and I can hear the hiss of the snowfall. It makes me think of standing in the yard where I grew up in a suburb of Chicago. When it was totally silent, you could listen to all those millions of snowflakes hitting the ones that had already fallen, making things quieter and quieter, more and more smooth. It's long after Christmas. I want to go home.

When I arrive, a gorgeous woman greets me at the door of what looks like a very clean apartment. She holds a Chihuahua, whom I try to pet so I can calm down, but who wriggles away instead.

"You'll work days," says this woman, who is neither warm nor unkind. "You'll be topless when you do the massages." *The ad said no sex*, I think. *This'll be just like when you modeled for art classes, except you'll make way more money and you'll have to be really, really assertive.*

"The ad says no sex," she continues as though she's read my mind, "because I don't want to get arrested, and neither do you. We don't do sex, but we *do* do—" She looks at me expectantly. I am supposed to complete the sentence. Her hand curls into a fist, and I understand.

"Hand jobs," I say, trying not to cry.

"Yes," she says, smiling. "You're sort of dainty, but you're smart," she continues, scratching the dog behind the ears. "The guys will like you because you're feisty. So we need to give you a different name. You look like someone with a *K* name, something hard. Katie?"

"Can I be Katherine?" I ask, thinking maybe I'll have more dignity that way.

"No, no, no," she says, irritated. "Sounds too bitchy, too up-tight. Now, can you be back tomorrow for pictures?"

I think of the pictures I've seen on seedy escort sites, shots of girls barely of legal age or made up to look like it that remind me of American Apparel ads, topless waifs looking impassively at the camera with descriptions like, "Petite and pretty, Tiffany will make your fantasies come true!" I've already applied for all the sex work jobs with more dignity, the ones without naked pictures online. There are a lot of model-like women in Manhattan who speak more than three languages, I have learned, and they are the target employees for the safer sex work. The sock animals I'm hawking in Union Square and on Etsy aren't selling, and out of the nearly fifty other jobs I've applied for in the last few months, two have led to interviews and none to actual paid work. I've lost twenty pounds and I can't afford my antidepressants without insurance.

"Sure," I say, looking at the wall.

"Great," she says. "See you tomorrow, Krystal. You'll be good at this, I can tell."

Down the block, I treat myself to falafel and try to convince myself this isn't a betrayal. *It's not that bad*, I say to myself. *Plenty of women do this work, and they feel empowered. Besides, you'll only have to do it once a week. The rest of the time you can look for other work. No one has to know.*

I do not go back tomorrow. A month later, I'm headed back to Tampa. I feel defeated, but I am lucky. If I'd had a kid to support, or a mother who didn't have the money to pay for the moving truck and the early termination fee on my lease, I would still be standing in a damp room off Twenty-Third Street, doing things that would break me and repeating my mantra:

This isn't degrading. I'm liberated. This is my choice. Everything's fine.

I didn't know it then, but my time in New York brought me to the end of my quest for hotness as power. I'd spent my twenties toeing the line of white female "empowerment," I'd played the game and paid my dues, and at the end of the day I felt smaller than ever.

It had also brought me to the beginning of my quest for a different kind of liberation. US culture had failed to give me any sense of real power. But a year after leaving New York City I found inspiration in a very strange place: at a Christian seminary, in a class on Muslim women.

CHAPTER TWO

"IS THIS REALLY ANY BETTER?"

Islam and the Couch Epiphany

ATLANTA, 2010

I am sitting on a couch outside a classroom at Emory's Candler School of Theology, a month into my seminary education. (Before I go any further, I need to clarify that *seminary* is a fancy word for graduate school of theology. I did not have a cassock, I did not have to give up sex or alcohol, and I have not, to this day, received a halo of any kind.)

Sunlight streams through the windows and cooks me, and I worry that my eyeliner is sweating off. I am sitting just so, so that my skirt (which pinches my waist) covers the tops of the knee socks I wore so that when I walked to school my heels wouldn't cause my feet to bleed. My hair, in a short, I-woke-up-like-this pixie cut, is arranged perfectly with fifteen-dollar pomade. My concealer hides my dark circles and blemishes, and I sit with my back ramrod-straight so that my tummy does not poof out and look fat. In short, this is just another day in the Suit.

I have just come from my Women in Church History class, where we had a guest speaker. A fortyish, stylish blond woman, she was there to talk about the modesty guidelines of Islam. This woman had spent some time in Iran with her Middle Eastern husband and their children, and while there she had covered her hair with a head scarf (hijab) and adhered to particular clothing requirements. Back in the States, she returned to dressing like she had before. When she spoke to us, she looked like I had when I worked on Fifth Avenue: styled hair, makeup, and professional garb. She wore the Suit too.

To a classroom full of vocal, educated feminist women who were eager to prove ourselves, this lecture might have been your typical Islam-slamming discussion on whose fault it is that men desire women and how oppressive the hijab is. I was ready to go to battle.

Instead, I was shocked into silence.

The speaker explained how much she had enjoyed dressing in accordance with modesty rules and also what a drag it was sometimes. She talked about her daughter, who had decided to wear a head scarf at age eight soon after returning to the States from overseas. She showed us a picture of her little girl, glowing in a neon-green hijab. The speaker passed around copies of *Azizah*, a magazine that calls itself "the world's window to the Muslim American woman," and the pages were filled with pictures of smiling, elegant women, with and without head scarves, and stories of their work as artists, activists, and academics. The speaker didn't advocate wearing the hijab—again, she herself was not wearing it when she spoke to us—but she certainly wasn't opposed to it.

This was not the podium-pounding, acrimonious discussion I had prepared for. Instead of feeling self-righteous and angry, I felt inspired . . . and profoundly unsettled. I didn't know it then, but what I had learned about Islam was teaching me about my own hypocrisy.

On the couch in the sun, I am reading *Muslim Women in America: The Challenge of Islamic Identity Today*. I am learning about women who wear the hijab. They talk about how covering their heads as part of their faith is a feminist act. They say they are insisting on being judged for something other than whether their hair is perfect or whether their butts are shaped just right. They are comfortable, they say. In a hijab, they feel empowered.

I look down at my own body, painfully encased in the Suit. *These women are more liberated than I am,* I think.

A still, small voice asks, *Could* you *cover your hair, even for a week? Could you go without makeup for a day?*

NO! You'll disappear! comes the panicked internal reply. Which is my answer.

I am twenty-nine, and the changes I've been noticing in my body—slight weight gain, a need for more sleep—keep me up at night. I wonder how I will make people listen to me if I'm not pretty. But if I really am that enlightened, shouldn't the idea of covering up be less scary?

In claiming that I found strength as a woman in organized religion, I realize that I am claiming something many people simply can't believe. Perhaps you are picking this book back up after having thrown it across the room in disgust or disbelief, the way I did when I realized that the Left Behind series was not just a fun book about people disappearing. That's OK. We're back now. Thank you for returning.

Here's a strange truth: in the years since I left New York, I have become a pastor, as in preaching sermons on Sundays, performing Communion, visiting people in the hospital. Believe me when I tell you that no one is more shocked by my life as a religious person than I. And before you throw this book again, know that this change from someone who thought the church was full of hateful bigots to someone who joyfully gets paid to do its work, has nothing to do with learning to be "pure" or reclaiming my virginity (it's a thing) or rejecting science or anything like that.

What happened was, the universe opened doors that I thought had been locked forever, and I walked through them. Let me explain how I got from behind a desk on Fifth Avenue to behind a pulpit in Silicon Valley.

. . . . .

Trapped behind my desk, right before the recession of 2008, I had a lot of free time. I spent about an hour a day restocking the pantry and answering phones, and the rest of the time staring out the window at the various Tiffany window displays as they changed from spring to summer to Christmas and back again.

I gradually began to realize that my life had become exactly what I didn't want it to be: I was working a job that paid the bills but was so exhausting and frustrating that I had no time or energy for doing anything I actually cared about. More dishearteningly, I'd come to realize that I didn't have the stomach for the film industry, whether I was working a day job to support myself or not. The #Metoo movement has brought open acknowledgment that sexual harassment and assault is endemic to "the business," but when I gave up on a career in movies in 2008, I thought I was just weak. I was never assaulted, but it was clear, everywhere I went, that things would go much better for me as a young woman if I actively participated in my own denigration. Job offers always came with dinner and drinks (complete with complaints about a sexually unavailable wife), older male authority figures constantly commented on my appearance, and I often found myself on the receiving end of humiliating jokes. It was just part of the culture. Many women can let that kind of thing roll off their backs; I'm not one of those women. I always took it personally, and eventually, the cost became too high.

The film industry wasn't the place for me—but what was? This receptionist job sure wasn't, and it was actually worse that I worked for a corporate ethics company. The company's job was ostensibly to make large corporations behave better; what we were, really, was protection against larger fines when those corporations got caught doing something unconscionable. We weren't making a difference. We were helping things stay the same.

So when I realized that moving to New York had been a mistake and I really had no idea who I was or where I was going, I had time behind that desk to reach out to someone I'd known during my childhood, someone who had helped me through my last life crisis. He lived in Ohio, so contacting him felt safe to me—in other words, there was no danger that he'd try to sleep with me. (I suppose he could have tried anyway, but he didn't.) It felt so safe, in fact, that it was like reconnecting with an old friend, only instead of it feeling like friendship, it felt like a father-daughter relationship. I started calling him Cosmic Dad. I even sent him a tie on Father's Day. I also felt safe asking him for support, because he had once been my pastor.

We're all aware that clergy are not necessarily better or holier than anyone else. In fact, thanks to the exposure of institutionally protected pedophilia in the Catholic Church, we're aware that religious authorities, like everyone else, can embody the worst kind of evil. But I'd spent my adolescence in Florida surrounded by really good people who were Christians, whom I really loved, who also thought that being gay was a sin and that their highest duty as Christians was to persuade other people to be Christians too. (Hundreds of thousands of gods being worshiped all over the world, but look at that! Ours is the Right One!) When I reconnected with my cosmic dad, he showed me, both by example and by recommending a mountain of books that came in handy during my postlayoff crisis, that faith did not require absolutism.

This caused a seismic shift in how I thought about the universe. I had majored in religious studies as an undergrad, because I love the beauty of the ways we humans try to connect with ultimate meaning. Truth be told, I also wanted some of that certainty, that *my god is the right god* feeling some of my born-again friends had. (I went to college in Tallahassee, the Deep South, where if you're Christian at all, you're a little bit Southern Baptist just because of where you are.) I figured that if I studied world religions, I might be able to settle my doubts about why so many Christians seemed to be so . . . unchristian. After a whole undergrad degree, I was no closer to that certainty. So, I figured, I might study religion, but I would never be able to enjoy it.

As I sat behind my desk in my sheep slippers, my cosmic dad answered my questions about all of this. When I asked how someone so educated (he attended the University of Chicago and has a PhD in theology) could possibly believe that anyone who didn't go to church was going to hell, he explained that he didn't believe in religious exclusivism—or hell, really—at all. He said that a lot of Christians thought that was medieval nonsense. He saw Christianity as one language, he said, among many for talking about something that's essentially beyond words. He used the Buddha's example of the finger pointing to the moon: spiritual teachings are the finger, and the ultimate truth is the moon. Confusing the finger with the moon is how humanity tends to get religion wrong.

But what about the whole evolution thing, I wanted to know. "Of course I believe in evolution," he replied via email. "There's physical evidence. I'm not an idiot, and my congregants aren't either. Just because evolution happened doesn't mean there's no God." He thought homosexuality was a stupid thing to fight over, since all people are created and loved by God the way we already are. He thought the Bible was holy, but certainly not inerrant or literal.

I gradually began to consider the different facets of my personality in light of what I now knew about what I was, and was not, willing to do for a career in film. I liked to care for people. I enjoyed studying spirituality. And now, as I read Joseph Campbell and listened to Cosmic Dad's sermons on the subway every morning on my way to my pointless, meaningless job, I had realized that faith and mystery were not opposites; instead, each gave the other depth. At the time I was vehemently opposed to the idea of becoming a parish minister, but since I'd spent my youth following Mom around as she did her rotations in med school, I wondered if I might like to be a hospital chaplain. Then I got laid off, which at the time seemed like a catastrophe. Instead, it let me leave a life that was no longer right for me.

When I got to Tampa, I enrolled in a chaplaincy program at Tampa General Hospital. I silently prayed over the body of a man who had just died with six bullets in his chest, while the whole ER held still. I held the hand of a mother with her son's blood on her shoes. He'd run out into the street in front of their house and was hit by a car going forty miles an hour. There wasn't anything to say, so I just sat on the floor next to her.

I stayed up all night with a family whose mother had been dying for months, and I was there when she drew her last breath and the family collectively exhaled. I was manipulated by drug addicts and got humiliated by a man who had absolutely no respect for women, especially young women in positions of authority. I learned the power of organized religion to heal, simply through the power of nonjudgmental presence.

I had never been so sure that I was on the right track. I wanted to go to seminary.

Which brings us to the couch after class, where I wondered if women in head scarves could teach me something about the nature of female power.

When Americans see a woman in a head scarf, we go right to a mix of righteous indignation and fear. *That poor woman*, we think, *made to be ashamed of her body.* Or we think, *Terrorist.* And what's wrong with feeling compassion for an oppressed woman? That's what we do here in America, where all are equal. And what's wrong with being vigilant? After all, at any moment one of those head-scarfed women could whip out a firearm and start shooting—never mind that according to the November 2015 issue of *Time,* one's odds of being killed by a young white man with the same gun are astronomically higher.[1] But the irreducible fact that Muslims make their women cover up is proof of the evilness of Islam, right?

That was what I thought too. But nothing about Western culture had enabled me to feel empowered—or even safe—in my skin as a woman. Nothing about modern America had given me value; in fact, I was convinced that I was only as powerful as I was pretty. That wasn't working.

Could it be that hijabis knew another way to liberation?

IN THE BEGINNING

Considering the messages about Islam with which we in the West are inundated, it's not surprising that we can't quite buy the idea that a hijabi could ever be a free woman. But what's at work is the misrepresentation of two ideas. One is that female exposure equals female liberation, a thesis I've already debunked. The other is that, based on its very text, Islam is inherently oppressive toward women. This is similarly false; such an interpretation of a religion with which many Americans are totally unfamiliar has much more to do with the West's long tradition of colonialism than it does with the rights of women.

In fact, Islam and Christianity suffer from the same problem: in both cases, men who came after the prophets weaponized the letters of the law to control women, when the original spirit behind the words was aimed at greater equity. The fingers pointing to the moon have been co-opted to support the agendas of those in power.

Sumbul Ali-Karamali, in her 2008 book *The Muslim Next Door: The Qur'an, the Media, and That Veil Thing*, explains how the prophet Muhammad's life and teachings sought to give women equal status with men. As an American Muslim who grew up in California, Ali-Karamali attended Stanford and holds two law degrees, a JD from the University of California, Davis, and an LLM in Islamic law from the University of London's School of Oriental and African Studies. The world of the seventh century, she writes, was not one that was kind to women. Common cultural practices in the ancient Near East included unlimited polygyny (the practice of a man taking several wives), a total lack of inheritance rights for women, and the acceptance of domestic violence, because women were considered to be male property belonging to their fathers, brothers, or husbands, depending on their familial status. The cultural soil from which all three Abrahamic religions sprang was thoroughly androcentric, if not actively misogynistic. Women existed to bear children, and not much else; baby girls were sometimes buried alive because they represented so little value for their families.

By contrast, the prophet Muhammad treated women as equals, says Ali-Karamali, both involving them in his life (not just treating them as heir machines) and issuing reforms that gave women access to property and social power. She writes, "He was known to often discuss political and social issues with [his wives], and they routinely offered him their advice. One of them, Umm Salama, defended the right of women to go to war."[2] Qur'anic reforms made female inheritance mandatory—*mandatory*—and decreed that women should keep their own property upon marriage, effectively reversing the common understanding of women as saleable goods. The Prophet "said the worst of his followers were those who beat their wives," another stance that directly contradicted preexisting cultural norms.[3] Bilqis, the Queen of Sheba who converted to Islam, became a Muslimah without ever being asked to "abdicate, give her property over to her husband, veil herself, and stay inside her house to become a subservient breeder of children."[4] Bilqis, a powerful woman, lost none of her power by turning to Allah.

Like the Bible, the Qur'anic story begins in the Garden of Eden—but *both* Adam and Eve disobey God directly, removing the "evil temptress" label from Eve and making both genders responsible for humanity's break with God. The teachings of Islam originally viewed women as human beings and not things, a unique—and disruptive—perspective in the Near Eastern world of the seventh century.

Much like Mary in the Christian faith, there are women in the Islamic tradition who demonstrate the often obfuscated but no less vital role of women. Many Christians and Jews know the story of Hagar, the handmaiden who bore a son to Abraham after his wife Sarah initially could not. What many do not know is that though Hagar is never mentioned by name in the Qur'an, her son Ishmael was the progenitor of the Quraysh, the Arab tribe into which Muhammad was born. She is honored in Islam as the brave mother whose courage helped bring the Prophet into being. During her time in the desert, Hagar ("Haajar" or "Hajar" in Arabic) is said to have run back and forth between two places seven times, desperately seeking water, before the angel Jibril ("Gabriel" in the Bible) caused water to spring forth at Ishmael's kicking feet. When Muslims perform the hajj, a sacred pilgrimage to Mecca and one of the most important rites of Islamic faith, they travel the one and a half miles Hagar ran (called the *sa'y*).

Then there is Khadijah Bint Khuwaylid, a wealthy business-woman who not only proposed to the much younger Muham-mad—in most accounts she is forty and he is twenty-five when they marry—but also enabled him through her financial support to become the spiritual leader he was called to be. (It should be noted that both Jesus and Muhammad were supported by wealthy women. To say it another way: neither the New Testament nor the Qur'an would exist without women.) It was not only Khadijah's money that strengthened the budding visionary; it was also her intelligence and character. When Muhammad was first called by God to be a prophet, Khadijah's response to her husband's unbelievable story was to encourage and validate him. As Tariq Rama-dan explains in the 2007 book *In the Footsteps of the Prophet: Lessons from the Life of Muhammad*, "This woman's role in the Prophet's life was tremendous. . . . When he came back to her from the cave of Hira, troubled and assailed with deep doubt as to what he was and what was happening to him, she wrapped him in her love, reminded him of his qualities, and restored his self-confidence. . . . She was a woman, independent, dignified, and respected, then a wife, strong, attentive, faithful, and confident; she was a pious Muslim, sincere, determined, and enduring."[5]

What might the Prophet have done if he had reported his religious experiences to his wife and she had laughed at him, ridiculed him, or told him he was imagining the whole thing? Khadijah believed in her husband's experience and message, so much so that she was the first Muslim convert. Like so many of us, Muhammad would not have been able to face his destiny without someone in his corner. As that someone, Khadijah played a major role in the birth of Islam.

This is not to say the Prophet's ministry was the antidote to the rampant misogyny in ancient Near Eastern culture, that Islam is a completely egalitarian religion that has simply been misappropriated. Millennia of male domination cannot be overturned overnight, even by divine edict. Even though Muhammad respected and advocated for women, ancient Middle Eastern cultural mores are still embedded in the Qur'an (as they are in the Bible).

Additionally, the examples of Hagar, Khadijah, and women like them, and the progressive attitude of Muhammad toward females in general, have been eclipsed over the ensuing centuries. Men who sought to continue their ownership of women have emphasized texts that support their aims rather than allowing their faith to transform them. Religion and politics have combined to codify into law the idea that women are less human than men. Something has been lost, and then perverted, in translation.

RELIGIOUS VIOLENCE

I wish I could claim that the consequences of twisting Islam in this way has led to nothing more than a subordinate role for its female adherents but, of course, I can't. That Islam is used as a justification for the brutalization of women today and that the Qur'an is used to force Muslim women to cover up are very real facts. According to Mona Eltahawy's *Headscarves and Hymens: Why the Middle East Needs a Sexual Revolution*, there is a "toxic mix of culture and religion that few seem willing to disentangle lest they blaspheme or offend....When it comes to the status of women in the Arab world, it's not better than you think. It's much, much worse."[6] A scary thought, since Westerners already believe things to be fairly atrocious for Middle Eastern women.

In Saudi Arabia, women were only recently granted the right to drive (it was said to be harmful to their ovaries), but they still can't go anywhere without a male chaperone, or receive medical treatment or apply for a job without a man's stamp of approval.

They are also prohibited from wearing clothing or makeup that shows off their beauty. Yemen is ranked the worst country in the world to be a woman, according to the World Economic Forum's *Global Gender Gap Report 2013*. Stories of the deaths of eight-year-olds on their wedding nights to much older men in the region "have done little to stem the tide of child marriage there," writes Eltahawy.[7]

In countries such as Egypt, the subjugation of women is often disguised as protecting or evaluating a woman's "purity." During the Arab Spring of 2010, female activists—those who marched in Tahir Square to depose President Hosni Mubarak—were subjected to "'virginity tests': rapes disguised as a medical doctor inserting his finger into the vaginal opening in search of an intact hymen."[8] Only the female protesters had to endure this punishment masquerading as moral judgment.

Ninety percent of married women in Egypt have undergone female genital mutilation, which can signify anything from removing the clitoral hood and glans to the removal of the clitoris *and* the inner labia and, in the most extreme cases, cutting off the clitoris and labia minora and sewing the labia majora almost totally shut. This mutilation is a concrete reminder that a woman's sexuality belongs to others (the elimination of the clitoris, the only organ in the human body thought to be solely for pleasure, is meant to curb a woman's desire for sex so that she "remains pure") and serves as a guarantee that a woman is a virgin upon marriage. Of course, in truth it is misogyny in its undiluted form, protected by a veneer of so-called concern for what is supposedly a woman's most valuable asset. It is also another iteration of the idea that a woman's primary identity is as an accompaniment to a man's.

In the context of this depressing litany of violence, injustice, and oppression of women, Eltahawy explains that most Middle Eastern politicians' concerns about women begin and end with making them cover up and disappear from public life. Both women who veil and those who do not are subjected to nearly constant harassment—and worse—by men, which is, just like in the West, so often blamed on how the woman is dressed. When Eltahawy was growing up, she says, a favorite aunt donned the niqab and was shouted at on the street: "'What the hell are you doing?' 'What is that tent you're wearing?' (Now in Cairo, thirty-four years later, such abuse is hurled at women like me, who don't veil.)"[9] Men often refer to women with uncovered heads as naked.

Eltahawy herself struggled with veiling and wore the hijab for nine years. Her description of that time is poignant: "I wore a headscarf for nine years. It took me eight years to take it off."[10] She wore it, she says, to protect herself from "the roving hands and eyes of men," but it did not help.[11] She was groped twice during her visit to Mecca at thirteen, once by another believer while circling the Kaaba (the most sacred site in Islam, toward which Muslims pray five times daily) and again by a policeman while kissing the black stone, another sacred symbol. When religion and sexual assault seem to be so closely associated, it can be hard to believe that there can be anything feminist about Islam.

WHY VEILING?

In reading about religious covering for Islamic women, you may be noticing a theme here: whether a woman wears a skirt in the West or a hijab overseas, how she is dressed is blamed for the poor behavior of the men around her. It's almost like clothing has nothing to do with it.

This is why voluntary veiling is a tool of liberation for many women in the West. If we are alternately slut shamed and then told that skin makes us strong, what happens when a woman refuses to play that game at all by covering up in a visible, voluntary way? The authors of the book I read on that couch after class, *Muslim Women in America*—Yvonne Yazbeck Haddad, Jane Smith, and Kathleen Moore—write that veiling is a way for Muslimahs to take back their power in the world as women of substance, rather than trying to adhere to impossible beauty standards. In the context of Western beauty politics, veiling is often a feminist act.

Veiling, as such, is an amorphous concept. No specific clothing is required in the Qur'an—no head scarves, no burqas. Instead, modern modesty guidelines are interpretations of verses that, as in all world religions, are flexible enough to allow for modification based on the cultural environment. These have to do with humble dress and decorum, but are nowhere near as brutally restrictive as many Westerners believe them to be.

Three verses in the Qur'an are most commonly used to support the practice. The first commands modesty for both men and women:

> *Tell the believing men to lower their gaze and to be mindful of their chastity: this will be most conducive to their purity—and, verily, God is aware of all they do. And tell the believing women to lower their gaze and be mindful of their chastity, and not to display their charms in public beyond what may decently be apparent thereof. Hence, let them draw their head coverings over their bosoms. And let them not display more of their charms to any but their husbands or their fathers or their husbands' fathers, or their sons, or their husbands' sons, or their brothers, or their brothers' sons, or their sisters' sons.*
>
> Qur'an 24: 30–31, from *The Muslim Next Door*[12]

Notice that the responsibility for modesty rests on both men *and* women, and that no "slut shaming" is involved. Also, no specific clothing must be worn. It is dismaying that the presence of a male observer makes such a difference in dictating how covered a woman should be. However, do notice that the only men allowed to see a woman's "charms" are those who are related to her and have a vested interest in her safety. Also remember that the world in which the Prophet lived was unkind to women, far more unkind than it is now—so keeping prying eyes off would have felt like protection and not restriction. The general directive in this verse is to keep one's body, whether male or female, to oneself and one's family.

The second passage reads:

O Prophet! Tell thy wives and thy daughters, as well as all [other] *believing women, that they should draw over themselves some of their outer garments* [when in public]: *this will be more conducive to their being recognized* [as decent women] *and not annoyed.*

Qur'an 33:53, from *The Muslim Next Door*[13]

Apparently street harassment has always been a problem. And while the responsibility-shifting undercurrent of making women responsible for male conduct is troubling, notice that here again there is no specific "you must cover your hair" talk. The emphasis is on dignity, not shame or the "evil" nature of the female body. Many covered Muslimahs cite this verse when explaining their choice to cover in order to be recognized as observant Muslims, women who want to be visible representatives of how a woman who honors Allah looks and behaves. Personally, I think that's beautiful and brave to want to represent your faith even though it may make you a target, as it does in the US. That seems like the definition of empowerment to me, to stand up to the same old white men who keep screaming over the airwaves about "the evil of Islam" by refusing to hide who you are.

Many, such as the Moroccan feminist Fatima Mernissi, believe that Islam does not mandate modest dress for women at all. Instead, as Mernissi explains in *The Veil and the Male Elite: A Feminist Interpretation of Women's Rights in Islam,* many scholars interpret these verses in light of their context and get a very different result. The original story in the Qur'an is that a group of guests at the wedding of Muhammad and his new bride were too rude to leave, and though the new couple was eager to be alone together, Muhammad was too shy to ask them to go. He was thought to be polite and gentle to a fault, and these verses are about drawing a curtain of privacy in the doorway between the newlyweds and their intrusive guests. Seen this way, the story is not about covering women at all but is meant as a testament to the Prophet's mild nature.

The point of these verses, it would seem, is privacy and self-protection—two values that seem to be in jeopardy already in modern America's digital age, especially for young women, as we are flooded with stories of revenge porn and exes who use embarrassing photos to terrorize us. Given that an important use of organized religion of any kind is to help one interpret the world around oneself, it isn't surprising that many Muslim women in America notice the constant tug to self-objectify and, as a result, choose to say, "No thanks," and back up their decision with the personal—and therefore no one's business but theirs—reason: "It's what God wants from me."

MUSLIM FEMINISTS

Today, there is no shortage of vocal, feminist women who veil. In the anthology of essays, photos, and interviews *Women in Clothes*, Muslim blogger Umm Adam explains how her beliefs are expressed by how she chooses to dress. Adam wears a *jilbab*, which is a long, loose dress with slacks underneath, and an almost waist-length head scarf, because she sees covering as a *right*, a way of asserting one's privacy, perhaps in a world that increasingly steals it. Adam writes, "I respect myself, my body is precious and beautiful, I know that, but it is none of your business. It is my private business and I respect my privacy and will allow only those whom I please to allow into that private space. . . . I have a brain and a soul and am an intelligent individual, and that's what you need to interact with. I have my personal dignity and space and you need to stay out of it."[14] That is the most feminist shit *ever*.

Muslim fashionista Zinah Nur Sharif appears on the cover of *Islamic Fashion and Anti-Fashion: New Perspectives from Europe and North America* in profile, in a gauzy peach head scarf that shows the silhouette of her lips and face but hides her hair and neck. Edited by Emma Tarlo, professor of anthropology at the University of

London, and Annelies Moors, chair of contemporary Muslim societies at the University of Amsterdam, *Islamic Fashion* is a compendium of essays about modest fashion, particularly the hijab.

In her interview with Tarlo, cover girl Sharif lays out the intersections between her creativity with fashion and the choice she made at eleven to wear the hijab. By her own account, she "never bought or even considered buying clothes from Islamic stores, as I do not consider them stylish or suitable to my personal style."[15] She would simply take Western clothes and make them more modest, gradually becoming a "style guru" to her friends and family. She began blogging on her site, *Zinah*, and presently draws inspiration from Tumblr and Pinterest.

Sharif believes that style is expressive of who one is. She does, however, draw a distinction between style as expression and style as selfhood: "Imagine turning up with a dress, high heels and a perfectly done manicure to play golf like Mariah Carey did? Now that is when you have crossed the line and being stylish has become your primary motivation and way of life. Style should be a secondary concern and should not take over your life."[16]

The positive testimony of covered Muslimahs can be found, almost without effort, on one of the most public sources of information in the world: the internet. *Hautehijab*, a fashion blog for hijabis, quotes the March 2015 Hijabi of the Month, Texan Leena Asad, as saying, "I feel that dressing more modestly has given me more self-respect and in turn, respect from others." When I maintained a blog about the Modesty Experiment, it had more Muslim readers than Christian ones, and on my Facebook page, the comments I received about how oppressive my experiment was are mostly from men. I have yet to get a nasty comment from a hijabi about how I'm contributing to Islam's maltreatment of women.

Of course, it's possible to wear the Beauty Suit *and* the hijab. Plenty of covered women never leave the house without a full face of makeup or obsess about their weight or their eyebrows. Modesty is not the opposite of vanity. But in the case of many hijabis, the choice to cover is not always a choice for shame. Nobel Peace Prize winner, and arguably one of the world's best-known feminists, Malala Yousafzai, wears a head scarf. Female Western converts to Islam outnumber men four to one—that is, women who are steeped in so-called progressive Western culture, where the influence of feminism is readily accessible, convert to Islam at a much higher rate than men.

It would seem that the common concept of a Muslim woman as weak, oppressed, and in need of rescue simply isn't true, nor is it the case that Islam is inherently oppressive to women. So why do we keep hearing it?

ORIENTALISM AND THE WHITE-SAVIOR COMPLEX

World Hijab Day, which began in 2011, is a yearly event that, according to its website, encourages people worldwide—men and women, Muslims and non-Muslims—to wear a hijab for "Better Awareness. Greater Understanding. Peaceful World." This is simply a consciousness-raising event to reduce Islamophobia (Miss Universe 2013, Carol Lee, participated in 2014), but the site is rife with vitriol, much of it from men, about the oppression of the head scarf. An argument one often hears on sites like these is that any woman who would wear a hijab, or a niqab or burqa for that matter, has essentially been brainwashed into wearing these things. And then someone brings up honor killings when a woman shows her hair, and everyone loses their minds.

This is a classic manifestation of a phenomenon called Orientalism. This term was coined by Edward Said, a Palestinian American professor of English and comparative literature at Columbia University, in his seminal book of the same name. Said uses the term to describe the way Western writers, explorers, and artists paint the East as a place of veiled (and somehow also hypersexualized) women, scimitar-wielding men in turbans, and Islamic fanaticism—in essence, fundamentally *other*, primitive, and, most importantly, inferior to the West.

Said writes, "Orientalism can be discussed and analyzed as the corporate institution for dealing with the Orient—dealing with it by making statements about it, authorizing views of it, describing it, by teaching it, settling it, ruling over it: in short, Orientalism as a Western style for dominating, restructuring, and having authority over the Orient."[17] Orientalism is a way of reducing and caricaturing Arab culture so that it appears to be nothing more than the West's shadow self, reflecting all the ignorance we Westerners have supposedly risen above. (It is interesting that these qualities were attributed by European colonial powers to almost every culture they encountered to justify both coercive missionary work and the institution of slavery. Perhaps the "other" isn't the problem.)

One central feature of American identity is the idea that US society is a free one. Whether or not this is true on the ground is up for debate, but the idea of our liberty to pursue our own paths is ingrained in the very fabric of who we are as a country. Because we in the United States are taught that no woman would voluntarily veil, when we see a woman who is covered, we see a fundamentally unfree and therefore *other* way of life. Instead of being just a piece of fabric with a million meanings and uses, the hijab becomes further evidence of Middle Eastern culture's backwardness.

Once a society is other, we of the dominant culture give ourselves license to judge it as though it is an object, a finite thing rather than a fluid phenomenon. And invariably, the other brutally subjugates its women (which should be a clue to us that the problem is not with other cultures but with our own obsession with policing the female body), most notably in ways *we* in the US would never do.

In this scenario, the covered woman is an object used to whip up self-righteous fury—which is why she has been seen so much more frequently since 9/11. Rafia Zakaria, author of *The Upstairs Wife: An Intimate History of Pakistan*, explains the intersection of clothing and colonialism in her essay "Clothes and Daggers." She writes, "Women's clothing is a powerful shorthand for all that is wrong with native culture and all that must be corrected by the empire [meaning Western culture]."[18] So begins Operation Iraqi Freedom. So begins the deposal of the Taliban in Afghanistan. So begins We, the Enlightened, invading countries filled with brown people because their damsels need our freedom, and how can liberating women ever be a bad thing?

Experiencing a passing pity for women under oppressive regimes loses the moral high ground when it is used in the service of dismissing or even hating the group to which they belong, especially if that hatred begins to morph into complicity with military action and violence. To claim that misogyny is confined to Muslim culture is mere projection at best and self-delusional bigotry at worst. The female body is almost always shamed, all over the world, and American culture is one of the worst purveyors of misogyny, precisely because its apologists refuse to recognize it.

I have established already that the choice-centered ethos of Western feminism is not as simple as it appears. I have also established that if freedom means social equality, the ability of women to support themselves with the same financial independence men have taken for granted for centuries, and, most of all, safety, then American women are actually far less liberated than those in other countries. Witness the data reflected in "The Glass-Ceiling Index" from the *Economist*, in which the United States ranks far below New Zealand, Spain, the Netherlands, and many other countries for working women's life satisfaction.[19]

In an environment in which women's worth is still judged by our physical appearance and not by our actions, covering can be a way to reclaim our power, to remove the tent pole that holds a whole dehumanizing values system upright. Ideally, of course, women would be judged on our personalities, accomplishments, and character. But we don't live in that world. Our options to assert our autonomy are conditional, and the condition of Western women is still, ultimately, that of objects. Covering robs the looker of the option to grade us—which is perhaps the real reason so many men are enraged "on behalf of" the women who cover for

World Hijab Day or explained to me when I eventually decided to dress modestly that I was completely misinterpreting feminism.

When I tell people about my project, they often cite a cartoon by Malcolm Evans. A woman in a bikini and sunglasses and a woman in a niqab glare at each other over their shoulders. The woman in the bikini and sunglasses thinks, "Everything covered but her eyes. What a cruel, male-dominated culture!" Meanwhile, the woman in the niqab glares at the Western woman. Her thought bubble reads, "Nothing covered but her eyes. What a cruel, male-dominated culture!"

ATLANTA, DECEMBER 2010

How?, I think. *How did I end up with so many clothes?*

As part of my blog for the Modesty Experiment, I have committed to laying out and taking pictures of my entire wardrobe, and by the third hour I am wishing I hadn't made such a stupid commitment. As anyone who has ever tried to clean out her closet knows, American women don't just have clothes we wear. We have clothes we used to wear, we have clothes we want to wear, we have clothes we have never worn, we have clothes we wear only once a year. We. Have. Clothes. Good thing I didn't even think about shoes.

Admittedly, my initial idea for what to wear during the Experiment was just cultural appropriation. I imagined floating around school in an abaya (a flowing, long-sleeved dress often seen in Arabic cultures), my head covered in a sparkly scarf, telling people in an airy voice, "I'm resisting being judged for my appearance."

But that would have been wrong, on so many levels. The point, I decided, was to stand out less, not more, and in Atlanta wearing another culture's clothing would have drawn the eye. Plus, I would have been trading my own culture's female costume for what would have come across as merely a *different* costume. That was not my goal either.

I have decided to make a few piles: one for clothes I can wear during the Experiment (no exposed shoulders or knees, not so tight that I have to sit funny, like that day on the couch), one for clothes I can't wear during the Experiment but I want to keep, and one for clothes I want to give away. What strikes me about my collection is just how many items essentially function as reminders that I am not as thin as I used to be. This, unsurprisingly, is not great for my self-esteem.

Once I have spread out a third of my clothes, I realize I just don't have the energy to get them all out, or the room in my apartment to photograph them all at once. So I estimate how much just this third is worth, and it comes out to about five hundred dollars. As a grad student coming out of two years of unemployment, I am horrified at myself.

The makeup and hair are a whole new project, a whole other day. Hours and hours I spend looking up how much they cost, categorizing each piece. Almost seven hundred dollars, and that's not including hair and nails. This is an enormous undertaking I'm finding I don't have the patience for.

I've already decided that I won't wear makeup at all, but this inventory of products shows me how central my hair is, too, to my sense of self. Preventing myself from having a hairstyle by covering my head is my chosen tactic for dealing with this element of my obsession. Hats, head wraps, and scarves are to be part of my new uniform from January of 2011 until my thirtieth birthday, in September.

In the last month of 2010, I begin keeping track of how much time I spend each morning on my appearance. With what I consider a minimum of makeup (spot concealer on my blemishes, lipstick, mascara) and without washing my hair, it's at least forty-five minutes a day.

On December 31, I get as dolled up as I possibly can. I wear a red dress, red lipstick, even fishnet stockings to a huge swing-dancing conference I attend in Asheville, North Carolina. I do my hair. I paint my nails. It takes forever. I feel fabulous.

The next morning, I get up. I put on the clothes I have selected for day one: a long-sleeved shirt, jeans, and a hat. No makeup.

I stay inside all day long.

ATLANTA, JANUARY 2011: DAY 3 OF THE EXPERIMENT

This is the stupidest fucking thing I have ever done.

I've gone out in public once since the beginning of the Experiment, in Asheville, so there's been no danger, so far, of anyone I know seeing me barefaced and modest. When I get back to Atlanta, it's been snowing and to my joy, people can't leave their homes. This only prolongs the inevitable, though, and on January 3 I must venture out for provisions.

Ordinarily on a day like today, when I don't have to go to class and I have nothing but time, I would spend an hour, maybe two, getting dolled up before doing my errands, because it's fun. Maybe I'll run into that scorchingly hot TA who sometimes goes to my same grocery store.

Today I slink around the produce section at eleven at night, in a slouchy hat, barefaced with a bad breakout. I actually check each aisle before I turn in to it, making sure no one I know is there.

This is the stupidest fucking thing I have ever done.

CHAPTER THREE

STILL NOT A NUN

How to Be a Christian Feminist

ATLANTA, MID-JANUARY 2011

I've been going slowly. I went to the grocery store and felt hideous, but I can't just hide in my apartment for the next nine months, so when my friends ask me to go out—as in, dinner and maybe a bar or club—I gird my loins and say yes.

It doesn't matter how I look, I think as I get dressed. *That's the whole point, right?* Getting ready to go out would ordinarily be my time to shine. I'd spend hours straightening or styling my hair, rock some winged eyeliner, and squeeze into some clothes that require a perpetually awkward stance to avoid tummy pooch. Tonight I put on another floppy hat, brown corduroy pants that look awesome when they're part of an actual outfit but look kind of sad now, and a long-sleeved T-shirt. The bags under my eyes are purple, and my lips are an inadequate bluish line.

It's humiliating.

I know for a fact that the only people who know anything is different about me are the friends I'm going out with, but in my mind, everyone thinks I am ugly. We go to Twain's, a middling white-bro brewery, and I notice that the waiter completely ignores me in order to flirt with my gorgeous friend, Noel. Not that I am always the most beautiful woman at the table, but I am unused to speaking to a straight man and having him look right through me. It may be all in my head when I ask a tableful of women, all rocking their respective Suits, if I can borrow a chair. They seem not to make eye contact when they explain it's reserved.

It gets worse when we go to a trendier bar. Walking up to the door, I can see all the signs of yuppiedom inside: highlighted blond hair cascading down backs, button-down shirts, the smell of expensive cologne.

"Oh, shit," Noel says to me, "I forgot my ID." I'm her designated driver, and by the time we get back to her apartment, we decide we're done for the night anyway. *Thank God*, I think.

Going out for the first time dressed modestly was always going to be hard, but that first night, I'd made the same mistake I'd made with the church: I'd thrown the baby out with the bathwater, as they say. There's a middle ground between Suited and sloppy, just as there is between evangelical bigotry and sneering atheism.

The Dalai Lama has said on multiple occasions that it's better to keep one's own tradition, and I'm pretty sure he's wiser than I. But how to navigate all the nonsense, especially as a feminist? Is it even *possible* to be a Christian feminist?

As far as many Americans can tell, Christianity is famous for all the wrong things. When Hobby Lobby was granted the right by the Supreme Court to deny in its employee health-insurance plan certain kinds of contraception to their female employees due to a religious belief that life begins at conception, the internet lit up with outrage about the conflation of religious freedom with religious tyranny (used, once again, to control women's bodies). The exploits of bigotry from the Westboro Baptist Church, whether picketing the funerals of gay veterans or spreading anti-Semitic propaganda, are usually rage bait; worse, there seems to be a sizable contingent of Americans who would willingly align with such views. When Jerry Falwell Jr. endorsed Donald Trump for president, other GOP candidates salivated with jealousy: the evangelical vote is a huge get for a Republican hopeful. Additionally, Falwell's support of Trump was an implicit endorsement, from a powerful Christian, of racism and misogyny.

The area of the country most closely associated with violent racism is the Bible Belt, and successful pastors are mocked and shunned if they publicly support gay marriage—which communicates to gay congregants that they are not welcome in the church.[1] Christianity is also tarnished by the xenophobia of the Crusades, the brutal anti-Semitism of the Spanish Inquisition, the misogyny of the Salem witch trials, and, of course, the mind-bogglingly awful systemic and long-standing protection of pedophilic priests by the Catholic Church. No wonder so many people prefer to be "spiritual, but not religious." The Pew Research Center reported in 2012 that the number of people who identify as "religiously unaffiliated" in the US is on a sharp rise (more than one-fifth of the country as of this writing, the highest in recorded history). And of those who identify this way, most are not looking for a church because, they say, "religious organizations are too concerned with money and power, too focused on rules and too involved in politics."[2]

I agree.

That's part of my reason for entering the ministry: paraphrasing Mahatma Gandhi, I want to be the change I want to see in American Christianity. That view of organized religion is also why I avoided investigating Christian modesty practices when I first undertook the Experiment. As far as I knew, Christian modesty meant nuns, Amish bonnets, or the admonition to women to dress in ways that do not make your brothers stumble. This last was the worst. I didn't need any more body shaming, thanks.

My views were both right and wrong. As it turns out, not all Christians are the same; it's just that crazy people make better headlines than grounded theologians. There is a significant movement among progressive seminaries and churches to move Christianity into the twenty-first century, and believe it or not, progressive

Christianity has a long history of abolitionism, feminism, and social justice work.

But I'm getting ahead of myself.

OUTRAGE SELLS

With the advent of the twenty-four-hour news cycle, news channels and websites have to come up with ways to keep us watching. One of the most common ways to do this is to find someone who grievously misuses religion. The reason is simple: the best way to get people to pay attention, and thus to keep us tuned in, is to piss us off or scare us. We get very angry when someone is supposed to represent goodness and instead represents bigotry, greed, or even outright evil, and the United States is full of people who call themselves Christian but who act in decidedly unchristian ways.

Our collective attraction to things that make us angry has been scientifically proven, multiple times. For example, in the *Journal of Broadcasting and Electronic Media*, the journalist and scholar John E. Newhagen explains the relationship between approach-avoidance responses in people—fight or flight—and images in the media. As part of his research, he exposed subjects to images that angered them, made them fearful, or disgusted them and asked them to rate whether they wanted to move closer (fight) or avoid the information altogether (flight). What he concluded was alarming: not only do we *approach* stimuli that anger us, but anger also *enhances* our memory. Fear is the second-most attractive emotion, and disgust generally causes us to turn away. In other words, things that make us angry encourage us to pay attention and then to remember whatever made us mad. Failing that, scaring us does the job too.[3]

So, of course, the story of Kim Davis, the county clerk in Kentucky who in 2015 refused to issue marriage licenses to same-sex couples, grabbed eyeballs. And of course, the Christian minister and former governor of Arkansas Mike Huckabee said that Davis's brief imprisonment for contempt of court was part of "the criminalization of Christianity," a ludicrous and overblown statement by any sane measure made to generate name recognition in his pursuit of becoming the Republican presidential nominee. In a weird twist of fate, saying stupid or offensive things in public no longer serves to discredit the speaker. Instead, the more bigoted and outrageous the statement, the more airtime (and hence profitability) devoted to the topic. Many of us were shocked when Donald Trump was elected president of the United States, but perhaps we shouldn't have been: whatever we believe, he either whipped up preexisting anger or manufactured new outrage, and all of America was unable either to look away or to forget what he said. In a bizarre feedback loop, the more we saw of him, the more we remembered, and soon what was "true" simply became a matter of what we'd heard before.

Also in 2015 was the Starbucks coffee cup scandal, when the internet lit up with reports from evangelical Christians claiming that Starbucks wanted "to take Christ and Christmas" off their seasonal cups by going with a plain red one instead of one covered with snowflakes and pine trees.[4] But this time, many Christians realized they were being manipulated. Pastor and missiologist (someone who's concerned with the church's work in the world) Ed Stetzer, in a *Christianity Today* piece entitled "When We Love Outrage More Than People: Starbucks Cups and You," asserted, "This is the wrong fight and being done in the wrong way. And, it's just making Christians look silly, like so many of these fake controversies do. . . . Don't get mad about stuff that doesn't matter. It wastes time and energy and hardens people to what you have to say about the stuff that *does* matter."[5] If *Christianity Today* is publishing articles like this, then there's a sizable contingent of Christians who are *not* Kim Davises and Jerry Falwells. One hopes.

This isn't to say that there aren't plenty of everyday people who hide their bigotry behind their religious beliefs. We have only to go home for Thanksgiving dinner (or become friends with someone from high school on Facebook) to know that homophobic, racist, or sexist Christianity is alive and well and vocal, with its cries of "God says X, and I believe it." But if we're looking at the Bible, God said a lot of things, most of them contradictory. Besides that, the Bible has been passed through so many hands, and been edited so many times, that it's ludicrous to take its culturally bound words and try to apply them as though times haven't changed. And even if God spoke *those exact words*, God spoke them in languages almost none of us speak—American Christians anyway—so how can we say that nothing was lost in translation? I've studied biblical Hebrew, and I can tell you: it's amazing just how much nuance disappears, even in the best translations.

So what's the upside of organized religion? If there's so much ambiguity, so much abuse, and so much craziness . . . why bother?

THE GOOD NEWS

Writer, anthropologist, and lecturer Joseph Campbell proved to be the doorway I was looking for into a less absolutist version of Christianity, one that had room for ambiguity. If you've ever heard the phrase "Follow your bliss," you've heard of his work. My cosmic dad recommended Campbell's book *The Power of Myth* to me, and my life was never the same. We commonly understand the word *myth* to be a kind of fairy tale, but Campbell, a pioneer in the field of comparative mythology, worked with a different definition. He believed that myths are "the world's dreams. They are archetypal dreams and deal with great human problems. . . . The myth tells me . . . how to respond to certain crises of disappointment or failure or success. The myths tell me where I am."[6]

Myths, then, are stories that help us understand the ultimate meanings of our own lives, a language for describing the indescribable. For example, in the hero's journey, the monomyth that Campbell believed to be common among all cultures, an individual must choose to undertake an odyssey in order to emerge into a life connected to ultimate meaning. Jesus, the Buddha, Moses, *The Matrix*'s Neo, Luke Skywalker, even Emmett from *The Lego Movie* all undertake the hero's journey, and with such uniform adherence to the formula that one can trace each step as the book, movie, or biblical story progresses.

How many people have compared pivotal moments in their lives to Neo taking the red pill (*The Matrix*) or "spending forty days in the desert" (Jesus)? Why do these stories resonate with us so strongly that we deeply relate to a little yellow toy (*The Lego Movie*) or to a teenager in space (*Star Wars*) as they receive a call to a greater life, refuse that call, are forced to accept it, overcome their personal obstacles, and emerge as something much more than they were? It's because these stories repeat a myth with which we are familiar, and that helps us contextualize and interpret our own personal journeys. Myths are not factual accounts, but what they give us is far more valuable: a way to connect with ultimate meaning.

All religions are built around collections of myths. The idea that all mythologies—religions—share common elements might have a diluting effect on the Bible's influence for some. What I took from Campbell's work, however, was that religion fulfills a sacred function in society. Every culture deals with questions of ultimate meaning and seeks to connect with something bigger than ourselves, and religious mythology is the best way we as a species can come up with to do that. That means I can understand the Bible as one of many myths, yes, but also as the one native to me and the culture I grew up in—and therefore the one most likely to help me connect with the sacred. It isn't perfect, but Christianity is my native spiritual tongue.

Now, all of this is great—mythology and its function, the hero's journey, the realization that Christianity is the framework that might work for my search for meaning. But where in the Bible does it say women are equal to men? Where is there a feminine God? How can a divine *he* (as it's translated) and a human-divine hybrid—also a guy—possibly understand what it's like to be female? How can I be a feminist and a Christian at the same time?

Well, I had initially hoped my Experiment would tell me. It did, but to be honest, it's hard to remember exactly what I learned—to be more accurate, it's hard to remember who I was. This is because a year after I completed the Experiment, my younger brother committed suicide. As anyone who has ever lost someone knows, death changes us, and I am not the same person now as I was before he died. His death blew me apart, and I learned another reason why religion is so important: it can help us survive a crisis.

ATLANTA, JULY 2012

The sun streams through the windows into the spacious, airy bathroom still steamy from my preclass shower. It's the summer between my second and third years of seminary, ten months post-Experiment. I had been feeling so good: the Emory alumni newsletter included an article about my modesty project. As far as I could tell, life did not get any better than this. I press the phone tightly to my ear to be sure I've heard my mother correctly.

"What happened?" I ask, sitting down heavily on the tile floor. This is the last of many calls I will ever receive about my clinically depressed brother.

"He was sitting by the pool at his apartment complex," Mom explains between sobs, "and he had a few beers and some Benadryl. Then he wrote a note, took a chair and his King James Bible into the pool, and drowned himself."

Andrew had attempted suicide almost every year like clockwork since the time he was eighteen, but some part of me always believed he'd get better. In the year or so before he died, he took to reading the Bible (something, to my family's knowledge, he had never cared for) and quoting Proverbs all the time. I think he was trying, the best way he knew how, to be a good person. I do wish I knew why he took his Bible into the pool with him to die. Maybe it was the only way he could feel closer to God.

I wish I could say that when my brother ended his life, I coasted along on a blissful bubble of "God has a plan" type of serenity. I was a newish Christian and I was in seminary; shouldn't I have been OK with my brother "going to be with the Lord"? As most people who have ever lost someone know, though, statements like

that—and the attitude they're (lamely) encouraging—can be ago-
nizingly unhelpful, or even make things worse. More than one
person has left the church because of such tone-deaf "help."

I was lucky, because by the time of my brother's death, I had
developed a faith that featured chaos and uncertainty as parts of
God instead of evidence of God's absence. Please don't get me
wrong: I retreated into periods of self-pity, bitterness, and too much
whiskey after Andrew's death. But never, not once, did I consider
the possibility that just because something awful had happened to
me and I couldn't understand it, there *was* no God. My theology
was flexible enough to include mystery. And for that I can thank my
seminary education, particularly the course on systematic theology.

Systematic theology is exactly what it sounds like: the disci-
pline of formulating a system of beliefs based on scripture, scholarship, and personal and historical interpretation. It typically deals
with theodicy (questions about the existence of and God's role in
evil), Christian anthropology (how God relates to humanity), and
Christology (who Jesus was). One could even say that when people
argue with their friends about how Jesus can't possibly be the only
Son of God because they don't believe in a virgin giving birth,
they're engaging in systematics.

When folks don't want to go to church because they don't
think heaven is the point of spirituality, they're doing systematics.
(As I've intimated, church is about more than that, but I'm simpli-
fying for the sake of argument.) Of course, there are a million different ways to do systematic theology, and in my second year of
seminary work in systematic theology, Catherine Keller's *On the
Mystery: Discerning Divinity in Process* was my introduction to one
of the ways, called process theology.

Process theology was developed from Alfred North White-
head's process philosophy, which reminds one of Buddhism: process philosophy posits that the essential element of reality is change,
not permanence. Likewise, process theology hinges on the idea
that while certain aspects of God are unchangeable—wisdom and
compassion, for example—God's essence is *living* and ever shifting.

God is not an old man in the sky who determines everything that happens to us; God is a lure that urges us to take steps of faith. God is change and challenge, creativity and the unknown.

Therefore, any attempt to split the nature of God into dichotomies (God is good and the world is sinful, God is male or female) falsely confines God to boxes, and God is by nature antibox. Additionally, God is highly relational, both concerned with how we treat one another and found in the bonds between us. Related disciplines include liberation theology, which holds that God is always both on the side of the oppressed and working for their liberation; and Womanist theology, which emphasizes the experiences of African American women, who find themselves in the impossible situations of double and sometimes triple discrimination, to reveal God's role as the one who "makes a way out of no way," as some black folks say. If you're beginning to sense intersections between process theology and feminism, you're definitely paying attention.

Keller explains theology as a "truth-process" rather than as a means to discover the capital-T Truth. This means that people cannot run around claiming to have the Truth and that those who don't share their version of Truth are going to hell. It also leaves room for the church to change positions, as it has done on issues such as homosexuality and women in leadership. As Keller puts it, "Discernment between ways better and worse, between the promising directions and the dead ends, never ceases. Theology cannot escape its own edge of judgment, not in the sense of an ultimate retribution but of a critical and self-critical truth-process."[7] If God is process and seeking, does that mean all we really need to do as Christians is be open to leading by the Holy Spirit?

No. This process of seeking truth does not mean a loosey-goosey kind of openness but a disciplined, serious search for God. The so-called restrictive framework of organized religion plays an important function here, and that's why I personally prickle at the phrase "I'm spiritual, but not religious." "Spirituality" can easily mean nothing more than doing what feels right without challenging myself to know why. It can mean no community to keep me

accountable, and no one to push me on whether I'm seeking en-
lightenment or just gratification. It can mean intellectual laziness,
opting for whatever comes easiest and serves *me* best, and then
backing it up with, "It's what I believe, and you can't tell me that's
wrong." In a world that's getting smaller and smaller, that kind of
selfishness can be dangerous.

Religious institutions, in their best iterations, provide flexible
boundaries against which we can test our convictions and include
people who will tell us the truth in love when we're using our beliefs in ways that are self-serving or destructive. Religion provides
accountability in our search for that which can never truly be
found but is always whispering in our hearts to keep seeking.

I am so glad I had moved past my "I'm spiritual, but not religious" phase by the time Andrew died, because I would not have
made it if I hadn't had religion to hold me up. Grief is also a process,
and my reliance on process theology reminded me that just because I didn't get it didn't mean there was nothing to get. The Bible
and my church community kept the essential mystery of my loss
from sliding into nihilism.

Aside from the humility I was gaining from having to trust that
God was not absent just because something bad had happened to
me, the people around me held me up simply by helping me to go
on with my life. I was angry, but I was in a class on Ecclesiastes—
passages from this book of the Bible are often read at funerals—and
my professor's willingness to wade through my loss and confusion
with me as I struggled to write papers about it made my pain more
bearable. I was sad, but I had classmates who were patient with me
when I randomly brought up death, again and again and again, in
class. I was a mess, but I had a professor who, when I emailed her
in the middle of the night that for some reason I could not think,
and therefore could not finish the midterm paper, replied, "You
just lost your brother. It's going to be hard to think, and to write,
for a very long time. Don't worry. Just do what you can." No one
said Andrew was in a better place, nor did anyone intimate that he
was in hell because he'd committed suicide. I didn't know it then,

but in seminary, surrounded by the faithful and the seeking, I was in the best possible place to fall apart.

Absolutes shatter in the face of calamity, but mystery loses its power to terrify us when we can interpret it through sacred stories. We can live alongside the unknown—which is the essence of God—as long as we do not insist on making our statements *about* God *into* God. To paraphrase Campbell, religion is useful insofar as it helps us be our best, most actualized selves. Religion is only religion if it helps us survive life.

PROCESS THEOLOGY AND THE SUIT

As I said, I am a different person today than I was right at the end of the Experiment. In fact, I had to completely restructure this book, because it's such a personal project and Andrew's death changed who I am. But as my reliance on process theology has grown, both during the grief process and after, I've begun to understand how useful this framework is for bringing feminist scholarship into dialogue with Christianity.

Many feminist theologians interpret the stories about female biblical characters like Esther and Mary in ways that give them a bigger, better role. This scholarship is sound and it's a powerful tool for many, but it no longer works for me. To me, the knowledge that the Bible is a very old book, written by very inspired men, in which many of the most important female characters have been obscured or written out, sucks all the resonance out of the idea that anyone therein could possibly be a feminist role model. It's not helpful, for me, to look at female figures in the Bible to help me understand how to be a whole woman today.

But if any tradition is worth its salt, it's *useful*. So can process theology help women navigate the Suit, or at least, help us loosen its hold on us? It can if we consider truth as a process and not an absolute.

Old tropes about women being naturally inferior to men because of Adam and Eve or that women are supposed to dress a certain way so their brothers don't stumble . . . these were relevant for the cultures and times in which they were birthed. It was not realistic to expect women to be seen as whole persons when their property and their very bodies belonged to their husbands or when they were not thought capable of having jobs that did not revolve around caring for their husbands and children. But now, as women make money and even have children on our own, for some reason, the inferiority argument still doesn't seem to disappear. Although so much has changed, women still do not enjoy equal safety or respect with men. Jesus's ministry was about equality for all, but women do not yet enjoy that.

So, can Christian feminists come at an ancient stronghold of misogyny—Christianity—from within, and change the narrative?

DOMINION

In the introduction to this book, I mention the way that admonitions to cover up women's flesh were often backed by the idea that God was behind the so-called natural order of things, and to pervert that was to go against God. Usually when women showed more flesh, be it ankles, hands, or collarbones, professed Christians would speak out and accuse women of sin, either via inciting sexual thoughts in men or by being vain. The following texts are among those used to support these restrictions:

> *Also that the women should dress themselves modestly and decently in suitable clothing, not with their hair braided, or with gold, pearls, or expensive clothes, but with good works, as is proper for women who profess reverence for God. Let a woman learn in silence with full submission. I permit no woman to teach or to have authority over a man; she is to keep silent. For Adam was formed first, then Eve; and Adam was not deceived, but the woman was deceived and became a transgressor. Yet she will be saved through childbearing, provided they continue in faith and love and holiness, with modesty.*
>
> 1 Timothy 2:9–15

Wives, . . . do not adorn yourselves outwardly by braiding your hair, and by wearing gold ornaments or fine clothing; rather, let your adornment be the inner self with the lasting beauty of a gentle and quiet spirit, which is very precious in God's sight. It was in this way long ago that the holy women who hoped in God used to adorn themselves by accepting the authority of their husbands.

1 Peter 3:1–5

And finally, a verse about veiling:

Any man who prays or prophesies with something on his head disgraces his head, but any woman who prays or prophesies with her head unveiled disgraces her head—it is one and the same thing as having her head shaved. . . . For a man ought not to have his head veiled, since he is the image and reflection of God; but woman is the reflection of man. Indeed, man was not made from woman, but woman from man. Neither was man created for the sake of woman, but woman for the sake of man. For this reason a woman ought to have a symbol of authority on her head, because of the angels.

1 Corinthians 11:4–10

It seems odd that the verses about how a woman manages her appearance are always followed by statements about male authority. Essentially the message is "Dress down, because you're inferior to men." What?

Yuck. What do women do with *this*? Can such a passage be redeemed or, at least, interpreted in a more egalitarian way?

Each argument about female modest dress in these passages has two parts. First, a woman shouldn't look too attractive; second, her appearance is based on her "natural" inferiority to men, particularly to her husband. Two of the verses cite the story of Adam and Eve as their justification for male superiority. Let's start there.

In the Campbellian sense, the story of Adam and Eve is generative and helpful, and its richness is part of why it has persisted for thousands of years. It's a story that explains why there is creation, as opposed to nothing; it provides answers for why we humans sometimes feel distant from God, why we have to work to survive, and why women suffer so much in childbirth. It explains why humanity has the knowledge of good and evil, and animals seem not to—or at least, we humans have an awareness of our mortality. In the ancient world, when the creation story was canonized, it also provided scriptural support for the existing cultural status (subordinate) of women. As I've mentioned before, the world of the ancient Near East, where all three Abrahamic religions were born, was thoroughly patriarchal. The story of Adam and Eve reflected this state of affairs, making it "natural" and saving those who believed it from having to question the social order (which is often another function of mythology: it justifies the way things are, thereby alleviating existential anguish).

Cosmic Dad used to like to tell me that a myth was a story about things that are true but that never happened (I think he stole that from Campbell). Many people, thanks to advancements in the scientific world, believe that the book of Genesis, though gorgeous and inspiring, is not a literal historical account of how the world came into being. Religions tend to be syncretic—meaning that they take stories and themes from preexisting traditions around them, as with the way the birth of Jesus was blended with the Norse festival of Yule. The Judeo-Christian creation account is a myth, and it actually shares a few elements with multiple Sumerian creation accounts, including a story about a paradise called Dilmun.

In the texts found from that civilization, Dilmun is described as a clean and pure place, with neither sickness nor death. The gods inhabit the land peacefully until the Sumerian water god, Enki, eats eight plants in Dilmun and ruins everything.[8] Huh: a perfect paradise and immortality, wrecked by eating the wrong plant. Sound familiar?

The creation account in Genesis is an appropriation of other sacred cultural stories that helped form the identity of a community—in this case, that of the ancient Israelites. As the Abrahamic traditions evolved, the story of Adam and Eve continued to help adherents understand the world around them and to feel they had a personal relationship with God.

Today, when the story of Adam and Eve is used to justify an oppressive gender hierarchy, those who wish to move beyond this framework have two choices. First, we can say that these are very old stories, created in a different time and place from our own, and that they need not be interpreted literally. This is a valid point. The problem is that this approach is not as convincing to religious believers as, say, reinterpreting the story itself in a way that supports gender equality. When someone says to us, "Feminism is subverting God's natural order," we can say, "But the story you're using to support that point is very old and no longer applies to the modern world," but they're likely to dismiss us. It's much more convincing to leverage the authority of the text they're using to support an alternative worldview. Either we change a mind or the listener is forced to acknowledge that biblical texts are not as black and white as those who weaponize the Bible would have them be. Either way, we have the vocabulary to describe a different narrative.

Rereading the story of Adam and Eve to support gender equality is shockingly easy to do, so much so that it's a testament to the force of cultural mores that the whole church hasn't yet accepted it as doctrine. Pioneer feminist theologian Anne McGrew Bennett, in her essay "Overcoming the Biblical and Traditional Subordination of Women," uses the creation story as a wedge to loosen the death grip of male domination in Christian culture. She starts with the statement in Genesis so often used to subordinate women: "Then God said, 'Let us make man in our image and likeness.' (1:26)." The Hebrew Bible has many words for God, and Bennett tells us that the word used here is not Yahweh or El, both of which are masculine singular. No, here the word is Elohim, "a plural word which is used in the Bible for a female or male God or Gods."[9]

Then this male-female entity creates humanity "in our likeness," male *and* female, perhaps each gender even containing elements of the other. When God creates us, God is not only not masculine but also multitudinous in aspect—hardly a man, creating a man who looks just like "him," and then making a woman as an afterthought. Bennett also claims that the translation of the word "man" in this passage "can be used in the generic sense and include woman. It is so used here. The Hebrew word in this passage is a generic term, not a male term. It should be translated 'persons' or 'humankind,' not 'man,' which may mean 'male' and always carries a male image."[10] She concludes this section with a powerful claim: "God's attributes are not limited and there are no inferior persons. Woman is portrayed the same as man. Both are persons; sex is secondary."[11]

The book of Genesis includes two creation accounts, and the other is also used to relegate women to an inferior role: the idea of a woman as a "help meet" (Genesis 2:18, King James Version) for a man. In this story, neither woman nor man is created in God's image, and the woman is said to be inferior to the man because she was created after him. Bennett points out—and I love this, and I will be using it every single time I have to have conversations about this, which, if my life so far has been any indication, will be frequent—that by that logic, man is inferior to almost everything else on the planet because he came second to last. If order dictates value, then humans are literally the least important thing God has ever created, after sloths and the sea and cucumbers.

Additionally, if one gender can't survive without the other to help them, what does that say about who the stronger gender actually is? Bennett tells us, too, that "the word translated as 'help meet' or 'helper' is the Hebrew word used for divine, or superior, help. The word never refers to inferior help in the Bible."[12] It seems as though, if woman was indeed created as a helpmeet for man, her presence is a conduit for God in his life and deserves much more respect than other interpretations of this passage have traditionally engendered.

Finally, Bennett tackles the story of the Fall, and when she has made her case, this narrative—which has been used for centuries upon centuries to justify the subjugation of women—is so feminist that I can understand why such perspectives have been suppressed by male authority figures for so long. Instead of the common interpretation of the punishment given to Eve after she eats of the forbidden fruit as having to submit to a husband's mastery over her—"I will increase your labor and your groaning, and in labor you shall bear children. You shall be eager for your husband, and he shall be your master" (Genesis 3:16)—Bennett explains that this passage represents a departure from woman's ideal state rather than a manifestation of a natural order.

Subjugation by a man does not reinforce a woman's contact with the divine; in fact, it lessens it. If that's not a condemnation of female oppression, *especially* by a husband over a wife, I don't know what is.

POWER AND TRADITIONAL MODESTY

So, if the story of Adam and Eve is not unequivocal evidence of male authority, how do modesty arguments that hinge on gender hierarchy hold up?

If they depend on women's subordinate status, they don't. They just don't. Note, too, that there's nothing in the original modesty verses (1 Timothy, 1 Peter, and 1 Corinthians) about sex or too much skin. Those are all human obsessions that have been repeated for two thousand years of institutionalized patriarchy. It's time to let them go. In the Bible, women are not made responsible for the thoughts and actions of men; we (people) have done that all by ourselves, and it's time to stop using faith as an excuse to repeat it.

Many churches, including the Church of Jesus Christ of Latter-Day Saints, use modesty guidelines to avoid "causing our brothers to stumble," a phrase that borrows its legitimacy from yet other verses of scripture. The first citation is in Romans: "It is not good to eat meat or drink wine or do anything that makes your brother or sister stumble" (Romans 14:21). Note that this verse is taken as a prohibition against dressing suggestively, and even drinking, but not against eating meat. Additionally, the term "stumble" is quite open to interpretation—it could mean anything from be-ing sexually attracted to someone to not resting on the Sabbath. Caution against making others stumble also appears in 1 Corinthi-ans. Nowhere in the Bible does it say, "Women, make sure not to incite lust in men. If you do, they can't help what they do next."

In fact, Jesus himself puts full responsibility on *men* when they look at women "with lust." And he doesn't just tell them to look away; he tells them to pluck out their eyes (Matthew 5:28). Some-how that verse is never cited in discussions about modesty. Paul, a human being who never met Jesus in the flesh, is said to be the author of every verse used to justify covering women; but when it comes to what Jesus actually said, it's the man's job to manage his own feelings.

Paul even says, at the end of his head-covering verses in 1 Corinthians, "Judge for yourselves: is it proper for a woman to pray to God with her head unveiled? . . . But if anyone is disposed to be contentious—we have no such custom, nor do the churches of God" (1 Corinthians 11:13, 16). In *The Writings of the New Tes-tament*, theologian Luke Timothy Johnson points out that "the intrinsic weakness of Paul's position is indicated by the number of arguments he must invoke and his constant need to qualify them"—the gentleman doth protest too much.[13] Female covering is not, nor was it ever meant to be, such a central tenet of the Christian faith.

My point is this: the cultures that have evolved into those of the modern world have always been afraid of female sexuality, indepen-dent of what any deity has said. Because they're so afraid, they use spirituality to make women into mere accompaniments to men, and in the same breath make us somehow responsible for men's thoughts and behavior. The methods used to support this egre-giously unfair and often violent worldview have often involved the weaponization of the Bible, but at this point in history many of us realize that supposed scriptural support—which is actually scrip-tural *interpretation*—does not automatically validate a point.

Even within the modern Christian tradition, enough people know that the church can't continue to stand on the wrong side of history when it comes to how women are treated. Either the institution shows its relevance and vitality by fighting for feminism and equality for all or the Pew numbers will eventually show that no one is "religious" anymore. Not in the US anyway.

ATLANTA, FEBRUARY 2011

I am preaching today at Candler's weekly worship service. *I am preaching*, and not a professor or an activist or an ordained minister, because as of this point I am a Unitarian (I currently belong to the United Church of Christ). Today is Unitarian Universalist Student Day, and I like public speaking.

In this second month of modesty, I'm already a little bored. Going outside without makeup is no longer a challenge. I'm now used to pinning on a wig cap over my unstyled hair, wrapping a scarf around it, and making a bun at the nape of my neck, or smooshing a hat on, tucking in my hair, and running out the door. Because I am appearing in a professional capacity today, I decide to wear a tiny bit of makeup. Concealer, mascara, and a little blush, and I'm ready to go.

I peer at myself in the mirror and realize something fundamental has changed. For the first time in my life, I feel uglier with makeup on. My mascara looks lumpy and fake. My cheeks look sunken instead of contoured. And my skin looks, somehow . . . *apologetic*, as though by putting on concealer I am admitting that I have something to be sorry for skinwise.

Let it go, I tell myself. *Your role today is not about how you look; it's about what you say.*

Since I'm feeling odd anyway, I decide to change up my look a little. Instead of knotting the scarf at the base of my skull, I pin the edges behind my ears and wrap the ends around my neck. Now only my face is showing.

I look like the freaking Virgin Mary in a suit, I think. *Or maybe a Muslim.*

I'm not wearing a hijab, but as it turns out, I look quite Muslim to the students at Emory. As I board the bus to campus, I am expecting to be stared at. Instead, people glance at me once and snap their heads away, as if they are afraid to look into my face. As I squeeze past people, they give me more space than I have ever been given in my life.

I try smiling at other women. They look away. In the reflection of the bus window, I can see them staring at my back.

At school, I skitter over patches of ice into the lobby. One of my instructors, Mr. Moore, is talking to another student.

"Good morning, Mr. Moore," I say brightly, shaking off my coat.

He glances at me but doesn't respond. At all. *That's weird,* I think. I have spent four months in the fall in a class with Mr. Moore that requires ten or so students to sit around a table and talk about our budding experiences in ministry. It's an intimate class, and I've had at least three one-on-one meetings with him during that time. Still, he hasn't seen me dressed modestly yet. I try again.

"Good morning, Mr. Moore," I say, closer and waving this time.

He stops talking to the other student with a muttered, "Excuse me." He smiles politely at me. "Hello," he says. "I'm sorry, do I know you?"

I'm stunned. Not knowing what else to do, I point to myself. "Lauren" is all I can think to say.

He keeps smiling, obviously uncomfortable now. "Lauren...?" As if to say, *Lauren who?*

"Lauren *Shields*," I sputter. "I'm in your chaplaincy group. I'm doing the modesty thing? You've had me in class since August?"

He blinks at me, looking into my eyes. *Come on,* I think. *You can't recognize my eyes?*

"Oh!" he cries suddenly. "Lauren! Good morning! I didn't recognize you." We're both relieved to have the end of this awkward conversation in sight. "You look so ... um ... so *different.*"

. . . . .

So, if women do not have to dress down in accordance with our "biblical" inferiority to men, that means dressing up *is* a source of empowerment—right? But that puts us right back into the Suit, and as we know, it's hardly good for us, nor is it all that empowering. The Bible does say something else, though, something that might help women live in better balance with ourselves and the world. And it does have to do with modesty, but not in the way one usually thinks.

CHAPTER FOUR

LESS G-STRING, MORE GUCCI

Christianity and Consumerism

TAMPA, JULY 2012

Everything awful seems to happen to me when it's hot. This is why I hate summer. For example, right now I am standing in the sweltering parking lot of a Mercedes dealership, with my luggage and an urn filled with my brother.

I don't want to go into the lobby, because it's clear to me that what I am holding is a dead body. *What if the lid comes off?* I think as I squint against the glare of a hundred luxury windshields. *Would Andrew coat these cars? Would he stick to my face?* Andrew would have thought that was hilarious, and before I realize it, I'm smiling a little.

This is our second stop after the airport. First was two hours at the hair salon: Mom wanted to get her highlights done for the memorial service tomorrow, and there wasn't time between picking Andrew up at the coroner and getting me from the airport to leave him (or me) at home. So, he comes with us to the Mercedes dealership, where Mom picks up the new SUV she bought after he died three weeks earlier.

Mom has never had a problem with expressing her emotions, but I would almost prefer her sobbing to her current state. Her disorientation is palpable. As we drive away from the dealership, she fiddles with the air-conditioning—but the car has so many features she can't work it out.

"I have no idea how the hell any of this works!" she hisses.

I don't look at her when I say, "I don't know why you keep buying all these expensive cars that are so complex that they piss you off."

She doesn't respond, and I feel bad for always being so judgmental. I am particularly bitter because I have learned, since the Experiment, that my principal methods of dealing with sadness—looking good and buying stuff—no longer work.

That the US cultural ethos—that is, our accumulation of goods and our obsession with youth—is unsustainable is not news. It's making us unhappy (nearly one-fifth of Americans suffer from an anxiety disorder, and almost 7 percent of us are depressed) and fat (it's well known that the US has the highest overweight and obesity rates in the world, by far) and is damaging the earth at a rate that, some environmentalists believe, will leave the human race without a livable planet in as few as sixty years.[1] Will Steffen of the Australian National University and the Stockholm Resilience Centre, after conducting a five-year study on humanity's effect on the environment, has said, "It's clear the economic system is driving us towards an unsustainable future and people of my daughter's generation will find it increasingly hard to survive. History has shown that civilisations have risen, stuck to their core values and then collapsed because they didn't change. That's where we are today."[2]

Many US residents know all this, and yet we fight to preserve the so-called American way of life. Why? If you think about it, our economic system is ingenious: human beings instinctively seek meaning and identity, and Western culture is built on the idea that goods can provide these things. We've learned to confuse ultimate meaning with what we can purchase, so when we feel empty, we can shop and temporarily feel better. We're so inured to this system that buying our senses of self online or at the mall seems completely natural to us. We also don't realize, until it's too late, that this way of obtaining satisfaction not only is temporary but also doesn't actually yield satisfaction at all—again, see the overall rates of emptiness and misery in this country. If stuff meant happiness, shouldn't the US be the most blissed-out country on earth?

I learned a different way during the Experiment. As a friend who was pursuing his PhD put it, "Christian 'modesty' was never supposed to be about sex; it was about ostentation. Less about G-strings, more about Gucci." Jesus was a countercultural, antimaterialistic man who cared far more for the poor than he did for fitting in, and Christianity (a religion that was started *around* Jesus, not *by* Jesus) has always been about simplicity, not accumulation. It's been co-opted, but Christianity can be reclaimed by those who know how. It's not the only way off the treadmill, but it can offer some powerful resources. And it should: economic inequality is at an all-time high, many families can't survive unless both parents work full time, and according to a 2014 study by the Federal Reserve, almost half of Americans couldn't come up with four hundred dollars in case of an emergency.[3] This means that almost half of us are living on the edge of disaster.

We can't rely on Wall Street or corporate America to do this work for us; the institutions that benefit from our fervor to consume have a vested interest in keeping us crazy. We also can't rely on the government, because until money is removed from politics, those few who are benefiting from collective American malaise are going to continue to keep the system from undergoing any meaningful reform. There are factors at play other than our obsessive need to buy more and more stuff, of course, but consumption as a way of life is a drug that sedates and blinds us—at least until we're forced off the treadmill by job loss, illness, or old age. By that time, we are no longer young, rich, or thin, and no one will listen to us anyway because we're no longer highly valued. The system will sustain itself until we decide we're too exhausted to keep going.

When I went modest, for the first time in my life I saw a way out.

HABIT: CHRISTIAN MODEST DRESS

When most people think of Christian modesty, two tropes pop into our heads: people who wear drastically different clothes from the rest of the population, like nuns and Amish folks; and young Christian women who may be indistinguishable from non-Christians, who are told by pastors and church leaders not to look too sexy. Most of us know less about the former than about the latter, but the history of religious dress is instructive: it shows how powerful clothing can be.

Contrary to the archetypical nun image of a woman in a long black robe and veil with white underneath, monastic dress varied—and still varies—by order. It is not a uniform handed down from the church, as some believe. The stereotypical image, which is sold on everything from puppets to plates, is not the way all nuns look everywhere; instead, it is culled mostly from the memories of baby boomer Catholics, 30 to 40 percent of whom were taught by habit-clad nuns whose orders required them to dress in mostly black with black and white veils, rosaries, and so forth.[4] In reality, habits have been made from every fabric under the sun, from denim to fur, and have featured diverse headgear, from the cornette worn by actor Sally Field on *The Flying Nun* to floor-length veils and even felt derbies. Each order has its own habit, and each habit was and is a combination of symbolism, practicality, and a response to the prevailing culture.

In the ancient Roman Empire, in which Jesus lived and died, one's appearance was regulated by the state according to station. Clothing served as a way of codifying and maintaining social order. Much like today, hair removal and dyeing, makeup, perfume, jewelry, and meticulous attention to one's appearance were a major part of ancient Roman culture. Elizabeth Kuhns, in her comprehensive history of Christian dress, *The Habit: A History of the Clothing of Catholic Nuns*, explains that secular Greek women wore a chilton (sometimes spelled "chiton"), "a voluminous and finely pleated, draped covering" made of "rectangles of cloth held together by pins or brooches and kept in place with a belt or cord around the waist."[5] Wealthier citizens wore fancier clothing, with "richly hued fabrics, often with decorative borders."[6] Poorer citizens wore plain white or natural fabric or dyed their clothes "a reddish brown, even though civic law forbade them to do so."[7] Veils differentiated married women from unmarried ones, and sometimes the type of veil told the viewer whether the woman underneath was married or widowed. Slaves and prostitutes were forbidden from veiling at all, and for a time prostitutes were required by the state to dye their hair blond. Finery and ostentation were everywhere, so much so that in the first century BCE, Roman laws were put in place to check excessive displays of wealth and status. (These were often ignored in favor of making statements about one's importance or sense of style.)

Early on in the Christian movement, one devoted one's life to Christ simply by seeking out a teacher and asking to learn from that person, as no formal organizing body existed. The earliest consecrated people who could be called analogous to monks or nuns—Christians who left behind their former lives and devoted themselves entirely to Christ—did not perform formal rites at all. According to Kuhns, "The holy habit itself . . . is actually older than any rites of avowal, which were not instituted until late in the third century."[8] The change in dress itself *was* the profession of faith. This is an early example of the power of clothing: simply changing one's garments served to reorient one's life and communicate one's new role.

That most of the earliest "religious" (a noun used to refer to monks and nuns) were women is can be expected considering the poor status of females in ancient Rome. Women of any age were legally classified as children and were required by law either to marry or to register as a prostitute. Among the many ways in which Christians ran afoul of the Roman Empire, however, was that many Christian women refused both these roles, believing that their faith required their virginity. Unless a woman was chosen by lot as a young girl to be a vestal virgin, one of a community of females pledged to thirty years' virginity while tending the Roman fires of state, this was not an option. But Christian women defined themselves by their spiritual life, and as such, they wore veils, though they were not married, to symbolize their unavailability to men because they were brides of Christ.

With these limited options available to women, it is unsurprising that most of the early religious were virgins and widows. These women were the first in ancient Rome to define themselves not in relation to marriage and motherhood but by their own spiritual life, and as such, they wore veils, even though they were not married, to symbolize their unavailability to men because they were brides of Christ. Jesus was a man, yes, but in his incorporeal form he was far less controlling or fickle than a human husband might be, and he did not legally own women as husbands did. This is an early instance, then, in which covering oneself symbolized rebellion against the prevailing patriarchy.

As the new religion took hold, communities who shared the same beliefs began to develop, and some began to codify how their members should dress. Submission to community guidelines was another way to die to the self, or subsume one's ego in the service of living a life totally devoted to God. Holy Rules, guidelines for the daily lives of the consecrated, were developed by church leaders and adapted, modified, and enforced by the abbots and abbesses of the community, who were sometimes the founders as well.

Certain elements of monastic dress have remained relatively unchanged over time, and each element is spiritually significant. The tunic is T-shaped, which is reminiscent of the cross at Calvary, as is the scapular (the garment that drapes over the tunic in front and in back, a kind of apron or cape, which sometimes has an attached hood). The color of the scapular denotes which community the nun or monk belongs to and his or her status within that community. Franciscans and Carmelites wore brown "to symbolize poverty and lowliness,"[9] and Benedictines were identified by their black scapulars; the Congregation of Sisters, Servants of the

Immaculate Heart of Mary, wore blue, "a color symbolic of the Blessed Mother."[10]

The color of the habit was often influenced by the ideals of poverty and simplicity, ideals that necessarily developed in tandem with the prevailing cultural mores and realities. For example, in Gaul, St. Caesarius (470–543 CE) recommended that monastics should wear only undyed wool, which would have been anything from pink to reddish brown, due to the expense of obtaining pure white or black fabric. St. Benedict (ca. 480–550) wrote that "monks [and the nuns who also adopted the Benedictine Rules] shall not complain of the color or texture of their clothing. It shall be whatever is available in the surrounding countrysides or whatever is cheapest."[11]

The symbolism of one's dress went far beyond color, however. Many orders followed strict guidelines about which fabrics to wear based on utility and climate, and everything from the number of buttons to the type of headpiece was meant to remind the wearer of his or her ultimate purpose. The Maryknoll Sisters of St. Dominic experimented during their development with practical solutions to problems like not having readily available head coverings when it was time to attend Mass, with everything from gray felt, derby-like hats to tri-pointed (symbolizing the Trinity) wire and cloth headpieces. By the time the habit was finalized, it included blue silk in honor of the Virgin Mary, a rosary "made from Job's tears beads strung on black fishnet twine by each sister before she received the habit,"[12] and a black cloak, which was worn at home in New York but not on mission work in the tropics.

The Brigittines of Sweden, founded by a Swedish mystic and princess named Birgitta (1303–1373), wore a linen headpiece "decorated with five red circles to symbolize five drops of blood from Jesus' wounds."[13] The Little Sisters of Jesus, founded in Algeria in the 1930s, wore denim habits, because they considered denim to be the fabric of the working class. Their veils consisted of a blue peasant-style cloth tied at the back of the neck. Often, nuns in a

given order would dress so as to make those to whom they minis-
tered more comfortable, donning the styles and materials of the
poor and peasant classes as part of their official habits.

For most of Christian history, joining a nunnery represented
an escape from the limitations placed on women's lives, especially
when it came to education and influence. Though nuns were
committed to lives of poverty and simplicity, most came from noble families whose members donated sizable quantities of money
or land to the order upon its acceptance of their daughters—so
though their lives were austere, nuns generally did not starve.
Moreover, highborn girls' value depended on their abilities to
marry someone who would benefit their families. Many of these
girls wished to avoid such a union or did not want to be chained
to lives of child rearing and domesticity (not to mention the risks
associated with childbirth).

Religious life offered an opportunity for an education, and abbesses—women who presided over a community of twelve or
more women—were highly respected. Their signatures often appeared on British Parliamentary documents from the eleventh and
twelfth centuries, and, according to Kuhns, "they were present at
all important national and religious celebrations and moved in all
of the same social and political circles as the highest-ranking offi-
cials in the land."[14] This kind of power and authority simply was
not available to women in secular life, even if one married well.

This is not to say female religious lived lives free from male
influence. Abbesses had no spiritual dominion, and every aspect of
life in a convent was subject to male approval in the form of the
leadership of the church. Also, as early as the second century CE,
church fathers began to urge women to veil or dress penitentially
because of Eve's supposed guilt. These men wrote extensively on
what female devotees should wear, often with heavy doses of the
shame-and-blame reasoning so familiar to women today.

Tertullian (140–230) may have been the first to use Christ's
commandment to "love your neighbor as yourself" (to paraphrase

with the NRSV wording) as justification for telling women to cover themselves, calling consecrated virgins "the devil's gateway" and deriding women for wearing makeup and dyeing their hair.[15] Women religious were still thoroughly under the thumb of men, but for many, a life of servitude to Christ and the poor provided an attractive alternative to one in servitude to a husband and children. In a narrow field of oppressive options, life in a nunnery was the most liberating for many.

One does not often see habited monks or nuns anymore. This is largely because the social movements roiling secular culture in the post–World War II years affected the church too. In 1962, Pope John XXIII called the Second Vatican Council with the aim of updating the Catholic Church's image and aims. Naturally, the utility and efficacy of the habit came into question. When all was said and done, the church decided that the habit was no longer relevant or particularly helpful, though it let individual communities decide what to do with this information. For some, the habit represented patriarchal oppression; for others, its simplicity and regulation were freeing. Some orders changed their habits completely; some changed them only a little. Many orders decided that the habit was an artifact of the past and did not serve them or their communities any longer, and they thereafter dressed modestly but without veils, robes, or outward signs of religiosity.

In another testimony to society's investment in both symbols and controlling women's bodies, many formerly habited nuns experienced hostility and even violence when they donned secular clothing, even though nothing else about them was different.[16] However, the world slowly adjusted, and now most American nuns dress like everyone else—perhaps a little more modestly, perhaps with less makeup, but without wimples (headgear) or robes.

BUGGIES AND BONNETS: AMISH MODESTY

I never seriously considered Amish dress for the Modesty Experiment, because it had the same problem as wearing a burqa or *salwar kameez*: it would have been inappropriately costume-y for me. I was not Amish, but people would think I was. Additionally, being in the Deep South and not the Midwest or Pennsylvania, I expected that people would stare, and that was the opposite of what I wanted. What I didn't know at the time was that in doing the Experiment, I was already exploring some of the values held by this unique community of believers.

Before the Protestant Reformation, infant baptism was not only a religious ceremony that was almost universally instituted; it also "determine[d] taxation and conscription for war."[17] Born of the union of church and state, infant baptism was at least as political as it was spiritual. Beginning in 1525, the Swiss Anabaptists, from whom the Amish, Quakers, and other Mennonites are descended, "rejected the state-church system that linked Christianity to citizenship and that routinely baptized all infants," believing that only adults could make a promise to live a life aligned with scripture.[18] The Anabaptists' refusal to obey the state-backed church resulted in violence that still colors the worldview of sects such as the Amish. Charles E. Hurst and David L. McConnell, in their wide-ranging book *An Amish Paradox: Diversity and Change in the World's Largest Amish Community*, explain, "The subsequent bloody persecution of Anabaptists, which is chronicled in both the solemn hymns still sung in Amish church services and in the *Martyrs' Mirror*, an eleven-hundred-page book kept in many Amish homes, created a skeptical and even fearful view of the outside world."[19]

Jakob Ammann, the man credited with starting the Amish tradition by branching out from the Anabaptists, was a tailor by trade who supported a stricter version of shunning—meaning to exclude the excommunicated—than the Anabaptists did. Ammann believed that instead of just keeping the excommunicated from the Communion table, they should be avoided altogether. This view of separation was too extreme for many, so he and his followers moved to the New World in the 1700s and 1800s. Interestingly, the Amish no longer exist except in the United States and Canada: the European Amish eventually merged into other Christian traditions.[20]

ORDNUNG

For the Amish, being a Christian requires a particular set of behaviors and customs, all of which are based in either tradition or scripture—most often, both. As with the hijab and the nun's habit, within the Amish community, dress varies according to geography and belief. In fact, insiders can tell what community someone belongs to by subtle distinctions like the length of a skirt or width of a hat. The cultural norms of a given Amish community (its *Ordnung*, loosely translated as a way of living in harmony with God's will) leave little flexibility within one's sect.[21] However, there are some forty Amish affiliations or tribes, each with their own *Ordnung*.[22]

In general, Amish people live differently because they believe that their faith requires them to be highly intentional about how they interact with the world. Stephen Scott, a member of the Old Order River Brethren, writes in his widely read *Why Do They Dress That Way?*, "Plain people regard the world as a hostile environment for the true believer."[23] This means that everything modern, from electricity to cell phones to clothing, is sifted through the community's filter of what is appropriate for a people whose focus is family, community, and God.

Because the Amish place so much emphasis on avoiding the worldly, almost everything about them resists American cultural values of individualism, instant gratification, oversexualization, and consumerism. Plain dress serves to combat all of these in its own way. It squelches the sin of pride and strengthens community bonds, allowing the wearer not to place too much stock in how he or she looks, and also signaling *gelassenheit* ("yieldedness" to God and commitment to the church). In some communities, mothers and daughters wear identical clothing, "family bonds expressed though clothes, a physical extension of lineage and love."[24] The instant gratification and breakneck pace of the fashion industry is scorned in favor of clothes that will never go out of style (because they are intentionally never *in*), and that will last for years, curtailing the flow of fourteen-dollar T-shirts from Target that ultimately end up in landfills or sold to rag mills overseas. Modesty for men and women is paramount, in dress and in conduct, and premarital and extramarital sex is forbidden.

The Amish are perhaps the most adept at avoiding consumerism, and all women's clothes, with the exceptions of glasses, shoes, and some bonnets, are handmade, repaired at home, and worn until they fall apart. The Amish do not *condemn* physical beauty or looking after one's appearance; it is the artificial enhancement of the body or the overvaluation of its beauty that seems unchristian to them. They prize cleanliness and neatness, scorning those who do not take care of themselves: "They see slovenliness as disrespect for one's God-given body and a poor testimony to the world."[25]

Plain dress is not only a way to resist the forces of the outside world, however. The Amish also know the power of clothing to define a group. Like many women who wear the hijab in the West, plain Amish wear long pants, beards, bonnets, and aprons because they are proud of their faith. Amish dress serves to mark the individual as a representative of his or her group, and many who wear it "voluntarily submit [them]selves to it so that the world can see we are a separate and peculiar people."[26] This translates into selective adoption: for example, their mode of dress is not merely a costume from a bygone era. Rather, as new fashions come along, the Amish evaluate whether it is consistent with their beliefs and adopt or reject it based on these criteria. Thus, Scott writes, "today some plain women wear a 17th century style dress with an 18th century style bonnet and a 19th century shawl."[27]

BUT WHY?

Of course, plain dress would not be so important to Amish folks if they did not believe it came directly from scripture. Amish clothing is an interpretation of many of the same verses identified in the previous chapter concerning modesty and proper adornment. Women cover their heads in response to 1 Corinthians 11:15, growing their hair long in further obedience to the text. (And yes, Amish society is firmly patriarchal, a point I will explore in a moment.) The Amish also avoid jewelry or adornment of any kind in accordance with 1 Timothy 2:9–11, which explains the absence of buttons and even wedding rings in some sects. The word "shamefacedness" appears in some translations of this passage, and that term makes frequent appearances in the *Ordnung* of many communities.

Thus far I have painted a rosy picture of the plain people, but of course, the Amish community is not perfect, and its environment is not one conducive to the kind of feminism with which I am comfortable. For one thing, if the Amish are wary of worldliness, then perhaps a connection between shame and femininity should be avoided. Also, in Amish society, gender roles are firmly delineated along boundaries that are irritatingly familiar. The man is the head of the household, and in public his family does not dispute him; the wife is in charge of all things domestic, and boys and girls are raised with these adult roles in mind. Some Amish men have jobs outside the home, but it is considered highly improper for a woman to seek fulfillment in a career.

However, some scholars claim that in private, divisions of labor and power are less rigidly aligned with gender. Donald Kraybill, senior fellow at the Young Center for Anabaptist and Pietist Studies at Elizabethtown College, and the foremost expert on Old Order Amish, and his colleagues write:

> Generally, girls help their mothers and boys help their fathers, but work is not rigidly gendered. Far more important than their specific tasks is that they learn to be obedient, work hard, and do their best. Thus, if there are no "big boys" around, a girl will take over some of the outside barn or shop chores. Similarly, younger boys may be pressed into service around the house, watching younger siblings, cleaning, helping with dishes, or working in the vegetable garden. If they have no sisters, the boys take turns washing and drying the dishes for as long as they live at home.[28]

Additionally, say Kraybill and colleagues, domestic partnership is meant to be just that: a partnership. The Amish follow a principle called biblical complementarianism, a gender essentialist worldview (and thus a problematic one, but it is what they follow). This principle centers on the idea that men and women are divinely destined to be different and provide unique and necessary elements to their partnership. For the Amish, a marriage is a mutually dependent relationship, and equal importance is placed on the role of men outside the home and that of the women within it. "The term *patriarchy* obscures a more complicated gender reality. Within the family, hierarchy is seldom absolute, and many Amish marriages are characterized by mutual support and an equality that is also based in Scripture."[29]

Though it should be obvious by now that I hold the plain people in high esteem, this complementary version of marriage and gender has been used too often to restrict women's lives to be comfortable for me. It relies on the idea that women *should* be interested in certain things and not others, exhibit certain characteristics and not others, and generally conform to very old, very restrictive gender stereotypes of the kind early Christians were often trying to escape. Given that the majority of those who leave the Amish are men—and, of course, because I'm not Amish—I don't think I can fairly judge the relative liberation of Amish women.

As I researched this topic, I was struck by the similarities between my aims with the Experiment and the stated goals of plain dress. Kraybill and his colleagues bring up an excellent point about the organizing principles of fashion, writing that the Amish "may appear to be obsessed with dress, but, ironically, they have fewer worries about clothing than do most Americans, whose dressing rituals signal obedience to the 'Ordnung' of Madison Avenue."[30] The paucity of choice is mentioned by several sources: if one can

wear only a few things, one is free to concentrate on other matters. Psychologist Barry Schwartz, author of *The Paradox of Choice:
Why More Is Less*, posited that the endless consumer choice most
modern Americans face is a major cause of their alienation and
malaise.[31] In dressing modestly, I was not aiming for communal
identity but rather trying not to be so defined by what the world
thought I should look like in order to be taken seriously.

In early January, at the beginning of the Experiment, a class-
mate pulled me aside, concern in her eyes. "Are you OK?" she
asked. She had noticed that I looked pale, and that no one had seen
my hair since before Christmas. Eventually I figured out what she
was saying: she was worried that I was ill. When I explained my
project, my friend was a little embarrassed, but it was sweet. She
was just checking up on me.

Amish women do not wear makeup, and one woman, who
gradually transitioned to an Amish lifestyle, experienced the same
phenomenon I did when she "went plain." In *The Plain Choice: A
True Story of Choosing to Live an Amish Life*, Sherry Gore tells a story
of being stopped by a fellow Baptist churchgoer in the parking lot
before the service. He asked the same question that was asked of
me: "Are you feeling sick?" Gore was as confused as I was until she
realized she was asked that because she was barefaced.

The churchgoer's reaction to Gore was very different from
that of my seminary friend: he implied that her interpretation of
the Bible as requiring women to "go plain" was outdated. Gore
writes that the man cupped his hand over his mouth and told her,
"You know what my wife says? 'If the barn needs painting—paint
it!'"[32] In this one conversation, he has told Gore that she doesn't
look well, that she's misinterpreting the Bible, and that perhaps
she *should* be wearing makeup. It's interesting to contrast this with
my seminary friend's reaction of apologies and encouragement.
The person in my story was a woman; the person in Gore's
was a man.

Begging the question, once again: to whom does the Suit belong? Your answer to that question will determine your answer to

this one: If men and women are truly equal, why do women still have to wear it?

OH NO! SHOULDERS! LAZY CHRISTIAN MODESTY

Perhaps when you think of Christian modesty, you think neither of nuns nor bonneted Amish folks. Perhaps you think of pretty young white girls being told by their pastors that part of being a Christian is dressing in ways that are unsexy or, at least, not intended to incite lustful thoughts. Or perhaps you think of online commenters using Jesus to shame women or even—and these are my least favorite—federally funded purity balls.[33] Whatever the example, the church is often known for an almost obsessive focus on promoting female purity through policing the way girls and women dress.

Feminists know how this reinforces the displacement of responsibility for male behavior onto the (exposed and apparently irresistible) shoulders of women, and how little sense it makes to shame the female body simply because men are uncomfortable with their own desires. In Victorian times, it was the exposed ankle or wrist that was said to incite lust, and in the 1920s, the knees were considered so sexy they were rouged. It seems that the only constant in the "cover up your X so I don't have impure thoughts" command is everything surrounding X. So why are there still so many red-faced pastors who spend whole sermons on the evils of an oversexualized American culture, emphasizing the shame of the female body rather than the shame of commodifying it? Why hasn't the song changed for two thousand years?

The answer is simple: aligning with the structures already in place is much easier than doing what the Bible *really* asks of Christians.

SEX VERSUS STUFF: WHICH MATTERS MORE?

The Bible has traditionally been used to back cultural norms of misogyny, but as I've discussed, the texts used to do so are not as black and white as traditionalists would have people believe. So what *do* these texts tell us, and why are we so loath to change our thinking in response? Let's look again at the original language:

> *Also that the women should dress themselves modestly and decently in suitable clothing, not with their hair braided, or with gold, pearls, or expensive clothes, but with good works, as is proper for women who profess reverence for God.*
>
> 1 Timothy 2:9–11

> *Wives, . . . do not adorn yourselves outwardly by braiding your hair, and by wearing gold ornaments or fine clothing; rather, let your adornment be the inner self with the lasting beauty of a gentle and quiet spirit, which is very precious in God's sight.*
>
> 1 Peter 3:1–4

Look at the words used: "gold," "expensive," "fine," "Do not adorn yourselves outwardly." What if these texts are not about sex but about conspicuous consumption? What if modesty is actually more about simplicity than lust?

One could confidently interpret these passages this way if there were supporting verses in the Bible, something about how materialism is a hindrance to faith.

Oh wait. There are. A lot.

- "You cannot serve God and wealth" (Luke 16:13b). This whole section is about how the things of the world are obstructions to God, how love of money and love of God are mutually exclusive. This statement is repeated in Matthew 6:24.
- "The cares of the world and the lure of wealth choke the word [the Good News, or words which lead to a spiritual life] and it yields nothing" (Matthew 13:22b).
- Consider the story of the rich young man who has kept all the Commandments to whom Jesus says, "'If you wish

to be perfect, go, sell your possessions, and give the money to the poor, and you will have treasure in heaven; then come, follow me' [meaning, become homeless like me]." When the young man can't do it, Jesus says, "Truly I tell you, it will be hard for a rich person to enter the kingdom of heaven. Again I tell you, it is easier for a camel to go through the eye of a needle than for someone who is rich to enter the kingdom of God" (Matthew 19:21–24).

- "And he [Jesus] said to them, 'Take care! Be on your guard against all kinds of greed; for one's life does not consist in the abundance of possessions'" (Luke 12:15).
- "Sell your possessions, and give alms. Make purses for yourselves that do not wear out, an unfailing treasure in heaven, where no thief comes near and no moth destroys. For where your treasure is, there your heart will be also" (Luke 12:33–34).

These are just a few of the sayings attributed to Jesus himself, to say nothing of the New Testament letters in addition to Paul's. Here are two examples:

- "Keep your lives free from the love of money, and be content with what you have" (Hebrews 13:5a).
- "For the love of money is a root of all kinds of evil, and in their eagerness to be rich some have wandered away from the faith and pierced themselves with many pains" (1 Timothy 6:10).

James, Acts, and Revelation also mention love of money as an obstruction to God, and the Hebrew Bible (Old Testament) is full of admonitions to help the poor and forgive debts. If Jesus were all about sexual restraint, then we'd see much more about the evils of lust in his ministry, not three verses about men's superiority over women written decades after Jesus died by a man who had a powerful conversion experience, a man who admitted to not being terribly sexually inclined. Jesus spoke about divorce and adultery, yes, but he was far more concerned with the allure of excessive wealth. So what's more likely: that Jesus was obsessed with covering the female body *even though he himself is not reputed to have said anything about it*, or that we're twisting the doctrine to support the status quo, the same way people have been doing in every religious tradition since time began?

Considering the realities of the modern world, I think that "modesty" does not refer to bodies. I think it refers to lifestyles.

BUT WE'RE NOT HURTING ANYONE

The US is a free country, it's said. Why can't citizens buy our senses of meaning if we want to? We can deal with our mortality when we get old, and retail therapy is pretty consistently effective. If it's working for Americans, why change?

Because none of us lives in a vacuum. With the rise of globalization, we all affect one another to a greater degree than ever before in history, and whatever each of us believes about what happens to us after we die, there will be generations after us who must live on the planet that we leave behind. The rare metals used to manufacture our cell phones sustain bloody conflicts halfway around the world, and due to the way food is processed, each time we eat a hamburger, the greenhouse gases associated with its production are equivalent to having driven 320 miles in an average American car.[34] The vegetables in our supermarkets are often picked by people who have crossed deserts in the dead of night in order to feed their families, people we'll probably never meet. We do not make our own clothes, instead buying most of what we own from companies that outsource their manufacturing abroad where labor laws are more lax, where sometimes children as young as five—whom we will also never meet—make our jeans and T-shirts.[35] The same thing goes for where most makeup comes from and the damage it does to the planet, due to both what it is and how it's made. And Americans' impact isn't just on people outside this country: remember the figures cited at the beginning of this chapter. We are both more and less connected than ever before to everyone else on earth, and everything we consume has a price, whether or not we personally pay it.

A new wave of religious scholarship refutes the idea that it's somehow God's will that humans use up the planet like it's ours to plunder. And now is the perfect time for such scholarship to permanently alter the church's environmental tune: as one scholar wrote, "Ironically, the greatest contribution the world's religions could make to the sustainability challenge may be to take seriously their own ancient wisdom on materialism."[36] The church has learned to survive by making itself into a saleable good; what would happen if church members used their influence not to accelerate humanity's selfishness but to help dismantle the system from within?

For example, in *Scripture, Culture and Agriculture: An Agrarian Reading of the Bible*, Ellen Davis writes that the Bible is not merely a book about spirituality but also about the care of the land as part of the life of faith. Davis debunks older traditional interpretations that the narrative is about humanity's so-called dominion over the earth, arguing that the biblical Hebrew root word and intent of Genesis overall combine to imply *responsibility for the care of creation*, not unchecked abuse of it. And humanity's job is not just passively trying to stay out of the way of nature either; Davis explains that in the covenant God makes with humanity, God has made the people *active stewards* of the planet. We are supposed to be cocreators and cosustainers of our ecosystems. In treating the earth as though it were merely an inexhaustible resource put here for our use, humanity is not honoring our end of the bargain made with God when we were put in charge of watching over creation. And this is only the beginning of Davis's argument. Due in part to the work of Davis and others, churches all over North America are greening their surrounding neighborhoods, heading up sustainability initiatives, and holding vegetarian cooking classes (since meat consumption is responsible for the vast majority of damage to the ecosystem[37]).

Or, directly pertaining to the reasoning behind some traditional modesty debates where "love your neighbor" means "make sure he doesn't lust after you," one could easily argue that since the Industrial Revolution, and especially with the invention of the internet, everyone is our neighbor. More conservative denominations have traditionally viewed the definition of "neighbors" in a parochial sense, but such a perspective is becoming less realistic. Are we obeying this commandment, which is repeated throughout the Bible, if we show no concern for those in sweatshops or mineral mines whose lives we affect? What about the way we treat the people in our communities whose cheap labor allows us to eat fast food whenever we like? If we look at the plethora of verses throughout the Bible about how we are to treat "the alien" (perhaps the most pertinent of which here is "The aliens shall be to you as citizens, and also shall be allotted an inheritance" [Ezekiel 47:21–22]), how can we propose deporting them or building a wall to keep them out? Are we loving our neighbor and being modest—that is, humble—when we refuse to share our excess with those who have nothing and meet their need with hostility and fear?

EASY FOR YOU TO SAY . . .

I recognize that my point of view is largely due to my privilege. I am lucky that I have the income to buy organic produce and the time to take sewing classes. But I am talking to the people who are like me: folks who take up a lot of room, who have the resources and the bandwidth to consider how our lifestyles affect the rest of the world, and who are willing to ask themselves whether we're living an outdated version of what it means to be religious. If the church is going to survive into the twenty-first century, it must be honest with its members about what "modesty" means now, today, in a world where our appetite for ostentation is causing harm to others and the planet with which God has entrusted humanity.

What I'm saying is, Christians should be leading the charge *against* consumerism, not coming up with ways to justify it.

I also recognize that change is slow to come. Global capitalism was not built overnight, and it's a worldwide system with far-reaching effects, most of which I'm unaware. For most of us, it's not logical to start a giant garden in our backyards or go campaign for workers' rights in sub-Saharan Africa or stop using laptops forever (I sure can't). We still have to live our lives. But what if instead of shopping at Abercrombie, we bought our clothes secondhand as a religious practice? What if one day a week women went without makeup to reduce global demand for it, because we're not supposed to overly "adorn" ourselves anyway? What if we made do with not-the-latest shoes *because we really don't need them* or skipped fast food for a month because it's bad for people, the planet, and ourselves? We don't have to change the world, but that doesn't mean we should throw up our hands.

This is not to say material wealth is evil or worthless. Many people over the course of Christian history have disingenuously idealized the disenfranchised, claiming that they (poor folks) are blessed because they have so little. It is usually a way to avoid sharing wealth, and it is not what I am calling for. Money buys housing, clothing, and food; it influences education and subsequent work opportunities, health, and life expectancy. Admonitions against the love of money go directly to the privileged, those who have more than enough and still are not satisfied. They go to those who can't let go of their old clothes even though they don't need them, because those clothes are who they are. They go to the average white United States citizen, but most pastors are not willing to say this to their congregations of average white people. When they do, the money dries up and another church closes its doors.

One of my favorite verses of the Bible comes from Luke. For me, it ties gratitude with responsibility. "From everyone to whom much has been given, much will be required; and from the one to

whom much has been entrusted, even more will be demanded"
(Luke 12:48b).

ATLANTA, JUNE 2011

I can't look, I think as I cram four or five pieces of clothing at a time
into a drop box. *If I look, I'll keep them.*

I've been dressing modestly for six months. At the beginning
of the Experiment I put clothing that was uncomfortable to wear—
too tight, or that forced me to sit or stand funny or suck in my gut
to look good—into garbage bags. My plan was to see if I missed
not having access to them. They constituted about a third of what
I owned. (Yessir, when a third of your wardrobe requires Spanx and
intense concentration, everything's fine.) I filled five forty-two-
gallon contractor bags with these items.

As it turned out, I didn't miss most of them. The pieces I did
miss and that were sufficiently modest for those nine months, I dug
out and wore. There were perhaps four of these. The rest I decided
to give to Goodwill.

But I get to the drop box, and the damn bags don't fit. So I
have to grab each item and stuff it in.

There's the Blue Ass Dress, so christened by my friends because it was covered in blue donkeys. I wore it on my eighteenth
birthday when I went out swing dancing, and all the best dancers
asked me onto the floor that night. I haven't been able to zip this
dress up since I was twenty.

There's the short, button-up red dress, the one I wore in a student film when I was around twenty-two. I sauntered across the
screen, singing, my long, blond hair done by someone else and my
eyeliner perfect for once. I used to go swing dancing in this dress
too, but the last time I tried it on, the shame I felt was physically
oppressive.

So many pairs of jeans that I wore on great dates but now I
can't sit in, so many blouses that I bought overseas or on vacation
that now emphasize my tummy, so many skirts that bunch up

weirdly around my butt. I realize that these are only pieces of clothing and that a changing body is part of life, and up until this point
I'd tell anyone who'd listen (and some people who didn't want to)
that a woman's body's natural aging process was nothing to be
ashamed of. But now, even though I've gained less than fifteen
pounds since I was a teenager, I find I can't forgive myself. I've
changed. At a size 8, I feel fat.

I take deep breaths and stare at the ground, transferring a third
of my wardrobe from the bags and giving it to someone thinner.
Younger. More relevant. *This is ridiculous*, I think. *Why is it so hard
to give away clothes I know I'll never wear?* I feel a little like crying.

When I'm done, I get back in the car and drive away. To my
surprise, I feel . . . lighter. Turns out, the hardest part was physically
letting them go.

There are good reasons why consumerism is called a religion—and
for that matter, the most prolific religion in history. It provides a
system of meaning: the things you buy make up your identity and,
like the Prosperity Gospel, the more you have, the better a person
you are. In fact, the United States even has a sacred Adam and Eve
origin story: that of the Founding Fathers. Their resistance to authority and supposed industry is the mold for the American mythos
that if one works hard, one will achieve material success, which
forever entwines consumerism with American identity.

Consumption also ritualizes our lives: we structure our time
and energy alternately around our careers and buying more stuff.
Consumerism as religion isn't all bad; it's made the United States
the wealthiest and most culturally influential country on the planet.

But it also makes us miserable, overweight, and empty. It's also
hurting the environment, a finite resource that many world religions before the arrival of Christianity viewed as highly sacred. It
also provides no comfort as old age and death approach, causing an
almost comical aversion to mortality, characterized by endless plastic surgery, marriages broken up for younger and younger partners,

and, as anyone who has ever watched a loved one die in a hospital knows, an absurd unwillingness to accept the reality of death. Our "religion," as we are finding out, is failing us spectacularly.

By dressing modestly, I took myself out of this equation. Knowing that I wasn't bound to "the Ordnung of Madison Avenue," I no longer felt like I needed to shop every few weeks to feel hip. Knowing that the newest makeup line I saw on TV was just the deliberate conflation of ultimate meaning with powdery chemicals, I felt silly considering the possibility that it would change who I fundamentally was. I saved more money because I wasn't hemorrhaging it into hair salons, and paradoxically, I worked out more because I liked myself: the model in the skimpy top no longer reflected my sphere of options, so I could ignore her.

Additionally, not having the option to shop when I was lonely or empty forced me to find meaning and solace elsewhere. I found myself crafting constantly, and while I recognize that this isn't a good option for everyone, I talked to God and read the Bible more than I ever had before. When I was bored I went out with friends rather than shopping online, and while sometimes we did get coffee or something to eat, because they knew I didn't want to shop, we often ended up in nourishing discussions about our lives rather than wandering around a mall. Sometimes I went out alone and people would ask me why I was wearing a scarf, and I would tell them. I never met a single person who heard about the Experiment and had nothing to say about religion, feminism, or the church.

Dressing modestly didn't make me better or holier or smarter; it made me more aware. Like habited nuns or Amish folks, modesty gave me the only ironclad excuse I've ever found to say no thanks. To all of it.

CHAPTER FIVE

TECH AND TZNIUT

The Digital Suit versus Jewish Modesty

ATLANTA, MAY 2011

"So you're . . . a *nun?*"

Oh good, I think. *This conversation again.*

More than halfway through the Experiment, I'm back at Twain's. (It's where my friends like to meet up.) This time it's not my imagination: I am being summarily ignored by every single guy in the room. Not just no flirting; it's almost like I'm furniture. I wish I could say I'm too confident for it to bother me, but I've just broken up with my boyfriend, and I'm feeling . . . vulnerable.

This strange reception has been the norm since I took off my makeup and covered my head: whenever I go to the store or a restaurant or anywhere really, most of the men who would have at least glanced at me have practically ceased to see me. It's unnerving. *Am I ugly?* I find myself wondering, more often than I'd like to admit. *Or do they just not see me because my costume doesn't ask them to look?*

Eventually, though, just the sort of dude who would have fallen all over me in the Suit strikes up a conversation. This guy, whose name is Greg, is young, white, educated, and a bit of a bro. He's also super cute.

Greg is the first guy I've ever flirted with while dressed modestly. I'm wearing a hat, a lacy blouse, and a skirt. Getting guys to chat with me has never been a problem—until now. Greg seems almost afraid of me. But he started the conversation and keeps talking to me, so things meander along awkwardly.

"No," I laugh in response to his question, trying to be patient, "I'm not a nun. Seminary is like getting a master's degree in theology."

He looks at my head, with my hair tucked up underneath my hat. "And you're dressed like that . . . as an experiment?"

"Yes," I say.

He stares at my beer for a second, then at me again. "So you— you like Muslims?"

"I—that wasn't the point," I say, smiling in the way I do when I'm reassuring men (*Why do I do that so often lately?* I wonder). "I was inspired because a lot of Muslim women say they cover as a way to liberate themselves. So I'm covering myself as a feminist experiment."

He blinks at me. He's trying. "So you're . . . but you're not a pastor or anything."

"*Fuck* no," I laugh, too loudly. I've found that I swear more often now as a way to say, "I'm not a religious kook!" The reassuring effect I intend is lost on Greg, though: he looks alarmed, as though a lightning bolt might strike him on its way down to me.

This bizarre interaction stumbles along, and I'm looking for a way out. Then Greg's friend mentions that they're going to a warehouse party tomorrow.

"Oh, fun!" I say. "I love to dance."

"Come with us!" says Greg's friend. *Oh no.*

"Is there a cover?" I ask hopefully. *This is how I'll get out of this weirdness*, I think.

"Twenty bucks," his friend replies.

"Aw, bummer," I say. "I'm a grad student, I don't have that kind of cash."

"I'll cover you," Greg pipes up, smiling brilliantly at me. "Wanna do dinner beforehand?"

What?

. . . . .

The next night, we three go to dinner; Greg covers my bill. I have
a scarf wrapped around my head, knotted at the back, and a cute
top, but tonight I'm in a skirt with a slit up the side (just to the
knee, but it's a little sexy). I realize two things: that Greg is never,
ever going to make out with me; and while most white men no
longer seem to see me, men of color definitely do.

Although Atlanta is racially mixed, people still tend to hang
out with folks who look like them. Twain's, for example, was almost exclusively white; at this awesome party, in a giant warehouse
with art on the walls and an excellent DJ, I am one of perhaps ten
white people out of the hundreds of people there.

In contrast to my lonely experiences at my regular haunts since
the Experiment began, I have a blast. I can dance here, whereas my
usual experience has been that the second I get out on the floor
people either stare at or try to grope me. People here are expressive
on the floor rather than overly sexual, because this just isn't that
kind of scene. I get many friendly nods, a couple of smiles from
guys. No one seems to simply not see me. No one buys me a drink,
but more than one attractive African American man yells over the
music, "I like your scarf!"

Greg, meanwhile, complains on the couch for an hour about
his ex-girlfriend, walks me to my car, gets in, talks to me for another half hour, and gets out. His friend tells me that the next night
Greg slept with some blonde from another club they went to.

Stupidly, I am hurt.

DOES THE INTERIOR MATCH THE EXTERIOR?

When people ask me how guys responded to me dressed modestly,
I generally joke that I made their heads explode. What I mean is,
most couldn't seem to understand how my external appearance
could possibly not line up with who they thought I was inside.
How could a makeupless, hair-covering, modestly dressed woman

act like every other woman they knew, most of whom they only ever saw in the Suit? (I know that's reductive, and I'm sorry, but it did seem to be what most of them were thinking. I know because I asked.)

To some extent, judging others based on their appearance is a natural human tendency. I would guess that this ability came in handy when humans lived in caves or tribes and one had to tell immediately whether an approaching person was hostile or friendly based on how he or she was dressed or behaved. We naturally make assumptions about who someone is based on external appearance. It's *what* we assume about them that is culturally conditioned.

Today, there's another layer, another exterior self, that women are expected to manage: our digital selves. Not only do we have physical bodies; we also have profiles and pictures in which to present those bodies, we take selfies and send short videos on Snapchat, not to mention whatever comes up when someone Googles us. These online selves rely increasingly on pictures instead of words: as I was informed by a twenty-five-year-old recently, "Only sad thirty-five-year-olds like you are still on Facebook, complaining about politics. The rest of us are on Instagram." This digital persona is another image to curate, an arm of the Suit that reaches almost around the world, and as tech becomes ubiquitous, attention to our online personas takes up more and more of our time. Between the real-life Suit and the digital one, women are encouraged to forget that we even *have* an inner voice.

We're becoming better at crafting online selves than we are at developing our offline ones. We spend so much time curating our images that, gradually, who we are online matters far more to us than who we are in real life, and the hollowing-out effect of the misogyny that permeates Western culture is amplified. After all, it sometimes feels better to get a Like from a stranger than it does to have an actual conversation with them. The Next Big Thing is often discovered on YouTube, where, as of this writing, there are more than eight million makeup tutorials, most of which are shot and edited by girls in their bedrooms. The proliferation of online pornography exacerbates the problem, combining constant exposure to scenes that portray women as playthings for men, scenes that are often accompanied by violence or coercion, with the expectation that women need to create an acceptable online self. And if the last twenty years are any indication, technology and online culture will continue to be the drivers of real-world culture in ways people today can't even imagine yet.

INTERNET FAMOUS

In her wide-ranging book *American Girls: Social Media and the Secret Lives of Teenagers*, *Vanity Fair* writer Nancy Jo Sales chronicles the lives of more than two hundred girls ages thirteen to nineteen and their relationships to the "dominant force" in their lives: social media.[1] One of the most informative stories she tells is that of attending Kim Kardashian's book signing in 2015 at the Barnes and Noble on Fifth Avenue, five blocks down from the office where I first dreamed of escaping the Suit. The book, *Kim Kardashian West: Selfish*, is a collection of more than four hundred selfies and nudes from the past ten years. "It was Kim naked in a bathroom mirror, naked in a bedroom mirror, clutching her naked breasts, leaning naked over a bathroom sink, sticking her famous behind up in the air; Kim leaning naked over a bed in the grainy dark, Kim in lingerie and bathing suits, lounging beside electric-blue swimming pools, doing 'leg shots.'"[2]

Amid the oohs and aahs of fan girls (and the "She's so hot" of boys), Sales chronicles Kim's rise, calling it "a perfect storm" of cultural forces. The American obsession with fame ("A 2007 survey by the Pew Research Center found that 51 percent of eighteen- to twenty-five-year-olds said their most or second most important life goal was to become famous. Sixty-four percent said their number one goal was to become rich"[3]), the advent of the iPhone in 2007, the acceptance of porn into the mainstream (Kim first burst onto the internet stage via what was asserted to be a leaked sex tape with singer Ray J, and, in a world of porn stars writing memoirs and appearing on *Oprah*, this made her into an idol rather than a cautionary tale), and the widespread popularity of reality television combined to birth the Kardashians, a family who's rich and famous for being rich and famous. Oh, and then they suddenly cared about trans rights when it was convenient for them.

Only a few years ago, taking selfies in the mirror was considered embarrassingly self-absorbed: witness GetOutOfTheMirror .com, a site where leaked pictures of flexing bros and duckface-pulling girls were posted and lambasted. Now, selfies and the various apps that allow users to take videos of themselves are so ubiquitous that cell phones have front *and* back cameras, and Kim has built an empire out of taking pictures of herself (with an army of stylists, but still).

A young woman selling a book of naked pictures of herself is nothing new. Madonna did that twenty-five years ago, and some people were scandalized, but it didn't mark a major cultural shift. The use of women as sex objects is hardly a new phenomenon, and neither is pornography. What makes Kim and the culture she's promoting so different is that in posting endless filtered selfies, she is championing a lifestyle of *constant self-objectification*, with both her body and the products she surrounds herself with in these pics. She's making her personal life into a product for public consumption.

In a study in the journal *Computers in Human Behavior*, the researchers found statistically significant evidence that online self-portrayal encourages self-objectification—in other words, when people present themselves online in any way, they are cultivating the habit of seeing themselves as others would see them.[4] Whereas before, women were merely exposed to thousands of ads per day that sexually objectified *other* women, we are now training *ourselves* to be the objects, and to see our skill at doing so as a measure of our worth. This is the logical conclusion to draw from the message that women must be beautiful above all else, and then giving us cameras and expecting us to constantly ask the world if it approves of how we shop, how our hair looks when we drive, what brand of lipstick we can afford. It is also the logical conclusion to draw from the fluency with which we can control our online selves. Who wouldn't want others to see them as they would like to be seen, rather than as the flawed, imperfect people all of us are?

At least one shot of me on my Facebook account is the product of more than an hour of prep. It's just me in my car, wide-eyed with good eyeliner, but it got more Likes than any of my other posts by far. (In my defense, I did not put on makeup *to* take a selfie, though some women do.) When I made it my profile pic, I got an even better response. And here's the uncomfortable part: I must have looked at the list of people who Liked my photo ten times. Why, even after the Experiment, would I *do* that? It feels good to get affirmation, but at what point does the affirmation replace my desire to accomplish my goals? At what point does the affirmation *become* my goal, and why, on some level, is that so tempting?

DIGITAL DIVIDE

Between the Beauty Suit and the Digital Suit, women are constantly reminded to see ourselves as products. Which would be fine, just a fun pastime, if this habit was not slowly widening the gap between who we are and what we think others want to see. One can straddle that gulf only for so long before one must choose a side, and the more time a woman spends on her digital self, the more foreign the terrain of her internal landscape may become to her.

Madison Holleran, the subject of Kate Fagan's *What Made Maddy Run: The Secret Struggles and Tragic Death of an All-American Teen*, was just such a young woman. She was a rock star in high school, but like many such high achievers, going to college meant suddenly being a small fish in a much bigger pond.

When she transitioned from high school in her small New Jersey suburb to the University of Pennsylvania, her main struggle was with her athletic career. She had always been a star soccer player, in large part because she loved to play, but to get into an Ivy League school, she'd accepted a position on its track-and-field team. She began to hate her new life: morning and evening practices for a team sport in which one is essentially isolated, in contrast to soccer, which is a collective effort. She didn't know her teammates, and she didn't enjoy running. Soccer had been what she did for herself; track was what she did because she thought it was what she was supposed to do.

During her first semester, Maddy became brutally depressed. What Fagan brings to the fore about this, though, is that online, Maddy had a perfect life, "as evidenced by the beautifully curated Instagram feed to which she frequently posted, documenting each wonderful moment after the next."[5] Maddy's parents talk about her relentless drive for perfection, her inability to accept anything less than an ideal image, but in conversations with her parents and friends, Maddy tried to explain that she was miserable and dying inside but did not want to disappoint anyone by falling apart or quitting.

Madison knew everything about how to control her external image, but when her internal world collapsed, she was bereft. As Fagan puts it, "The wilderness of her internal life, the constant waves threatening to overwhelm her, was her terrain—and hers alone—to navigate."[6] Her parents and friends tried their best to help her, of course. Her parents had her come stay with them and found professional help for her. They urged her to quit the track team to lessen her stress. But on January 17, 2014, Madison killed herself, leaving a community of family and friends behind who could not understand how someone who seemed so OK had been so completely not.

The contrast between the precisely controlled narrative of Madison's online persona and her internal chaos is not a coincidence, says Fagan. The more people curate, the unhappier we become. Fagan offers the insight that for the generation who has never known a world without social media, the internet is "fostering an increased dependence on outside validation, and consequently a decreased ability to soothe themselves."[7] When I was a teenager I would consume massive quantities of chocolate to get a dopamine boost, but if I were a teen today, I could get that with a few hours spent working on my blog on Tumblr. Why would I *want* to face my feelings when I could just make everyone else think I was perfect? Paradoxically, spending all that time on our digital selves actually makes us lonelier . . . but it *is* easier than engaging with real life.

The pressure on women and girls to curate the perfect online self is immense. Twenty-first-century American women have endured increasing pressure to conform to some strict feminine ideal as we've become more publicly visible (this is not a coincidence) and now, with the imperative of creating online personas that we know will be judged primarily by how we look, we have no excuse not to be, perfect at least in cyberspace.[8]

THEIR PORN, OUR SELVES

Alongside the proliferation of social media, technology has made something else ubiquitous: video (already an outdated term) pornography. I myself am not against pornography, but it does bother me that I can't even Google words like "porn" and "breasts" if *I* want to watch it, because what greets me are images and themes so clearly meant to dehumanize women that any arousal I may feel is instantly crushed. If I don't want to be disgusted, I have to type in some code words, like "consensual" and "definitely not a minor." Exposure to pornography—or at least the kind one tends to see on the internet, with a guy jackhammering away on a bored-looking blonde with a ball gag in her mouth, or videos with titles like *DaughterSwap* and *Teenfidelity*—*Stepdad Fills Lucy Doll's Pussy with Cum While Mommy's Away* (in which the real live girl, not a doll, looks *maybe* thirteen)—is almost unavoidable online. The creepy titles above are not anomalous; they're pulled from the homepage of PornHub.com, one of the most-trafficked porn sites on the web.

What's problematic isn't that there's so much sex available to anyone who cares to look; it's that what qualifies as mainstream porn is horrifying when viewed from the perspective of the woman. She's made up to look underage, she's being tied down, she's passed out (which the sites always claim is just fantasy), but most of all, she really isn't enjoying herself—and for a lot of porn, that's actually the *point*. It's disturbing because the message is that if the woman is *not* dehumanized or taken advantage of in some way during sex, then it's abnormal. At best, it looks and sounds like the only reason she's doing this is because he wants to; somehow her desires are a nonissue.

Given this constant exposure to porn as a way of life (and given human nature), it's not surprising that pornography's influence has seeped into the ways women self-objectify on social media. It's a short leap between online sex saturation and self-porning, and so, much of online self-curation consists of poses and expressions modeled on things seen on PornHub and Xtube. And as most people are aware by now, the effort to keep online porn away from anyone under eighteen is pointless. Forty-two percent of children and teens ages ten to seventeen are exposed to online pornography per year, with 66 percent of these claiming it was "only unwanted exposure."[9] These are self-reported statistics, so if the numbers are inaccurate they're likely to be higher in the former category and lower in the latter.

THE GHOST IN THE SHELL

According to the Pew Research Center, teen girls are the most frequent users of social media.[10] The teen years are notoriously tumultuous because the human brain is developing, forming new connections and pruning old ones at a rate that the National Institute of Mental Health claims is even higher than that of early childhood and will never be equaled again in one's lifetime.[11] We are, when we are teens, becoming ourselves, forming the values and identities that will carry us through the rest of our lives. In fact, says NIMH, "the capacity of a person to learn will never be greater than during adolescence."[12]

If we're learning at the highest rates of our lives when we're teens, what are young women who are steeped in a culture of self-objectification—not just sexual self-objectification but also cultivating the habit of seeing oneself as a product for consumption by others—learning? How would they know that the ball-gagged blonde, the drugged party girl, the stepdaughter wearing Chuck Taylors, even *have* desires? Because if they did, why would the men around them be gleefully ignoring them, and why would this kind of porn be so socially acceptable? Which would they choose to invest in, given what they're rewarded for online: themselves as products or themselves as people?

In 2007, the year the iPhone came out, and less than a year after the introduction of Facebook (consider how much technology has advanced even since then), the American Psychological Association did a study on American culture's sexualization of girls, particularly online. They found that "self-objectification in a culture in which a woman is a 'good object' when she meets the salient cultural standard of 'sexy' leads girls to evaluate and control their own bodies more in terms of their sexual desirability to others than in terms of their own desires, health, wellness, achievements, or competence."[13]

This means that through porn and social media, girls learn to view their own bodies as others' possessions—that is, what others want from their bodies is more important than what the girls want for themselves. There is a divorcing of the body and the self, a dissociation, that is required of young women. "Girls are forced to make a tragic choice: to capitulate to norms of femininity and dissociate from their true thoughts and feelings [to see their value as primarily as objects] or to resist this framing of who they are and the 'reality' in which they live."[14] I know very few adult women, let alone teenage girls hungry for acceptance, with the

courage to go against their entire culture even if they know it's
hurting them.

BUT IT'S SELF-SEXUALIZATION

Then again, the girls who post these pictures are not forced to do
so, goes the argument. And it feels good, when we are fifteen, to
believe we have the world on a string because we are beautiful, and
that this self-objectification is an acceptable way to order our lives.
Can selfie culture, and the porniness on which it runs, be
empowering?

As with most questions of female liberation, it's a complicated
issue. As one blogger quipped after Kim posted to her Instagram
yet another photo set of her grasping her naked breasts in a mirror,
"Dear Kim. Please stop using the term 'empowerment' when you
really mean 'marketing.'"[15] Kim frequently conflates "I am something you can buy" with "I am a strong woman." It's fine to use
one's body to make money, but as I've covered repeatedly in this
book, empowerment and nudity are *not* synonyms, and besides,
most young girls who self-sexualize are not being paid to do so.
They're doing it because it represents social currency or power, not
knowing that there's a price *they're* paying.

This price often becomes apparent, though, when the pictures
are redistributed without the consent of the person photographed.
In the past ten years, as smartphones have become integral to modern life, there's been an epidemic of stolen nudes being posted as a
way to bully, to make money, or just to attract viewers. (This is another, highly popular subgenre of porn: "Busty teen hidden camera!" is a typical caption.) High schools in particular are affected:
the last decade has seen a rash of cases of "sexting rings," in which
pictures that were generally not meant for public consumption—
usually nudes sent by young girls to young men they are dating or
hope to date—are aggregated and distributed without the consent
of the subjects.[16] That the term "revenge porn" even exists, and

that internet giants like Google are having to enact software to combat it, should remove any doubt about the usefulness of online self-sexualization as a method of empowerment.

This is not to say that, as teenagers, girls obsess about how we look and what boys think of us simply because pop culture foists these values upon us. There is truth to the idea that we are biologically wired to do so, largely because we are most fertile during adolescence. Louann Brizendine, a neuropsychiatrist at the University of California, San Francisco, explains that "whether the media were there to influence their self-image or not . . . [teenage girls] would be obsessing over whether or not boys thought they looked good because their hormones create the reality in their brains that being attractive to boys is the most important thing."[17]

But if this force is built into us evolutionarily, is that a sufficient excuse for exploiting it? Both the kings and the beneficiaries of the tech revolution are almost exclusively male, and it would be ludicrous to suggest that those both running the companies and consuming the content would not have a vested interest in maintaining their social dominance. With 79 percent of Twitter's leadership team being male and Google struggling to mitigate the damage from leaked employee emails about how women are not *naturally* suited to tech, those at the helm of the electronic revolution are presumably not interested in the effects of constant online female objectification—not because they're bad people but because it simply doesn't affect them.[18] Not adversely, anyway.

As a resident of Silicon Valley and the partner of someone who works in tech, I can confirm that the world of the internet is dominated by entitled young men, most of whom are white and wealthy, who generally treat women with such scorn that it's unsettling—again, not because they're evil, but because they *can*. Additionally, if young women are wired to care so much about what boys think, does that really need to be augmented online? Can't we spend our time on something else, since we're already sufficiently equipped by Mother Nature to continue the species?

Women and girls between the ages of, say, sixteen and thirty are carving out their spaces in life. They're committing to causes, figuring out whether they want families and with whom. They're changing cities, changing jobs, figuring out who they are internally. But if you've been groomed to believe, for your entire adolescence, that your greatest goal is getting more followers on Instagram or subscribers on YouTube, then you are spending that time obsessing about your image—the Digital Suit—and drifting away from your internal self while you do. In fact, the better you are at ignoring your personhood, the more effectively you're able to make yourself into an internet object. The boys, meanwhile, are learning to get by in a world that values only one thing over youth—material success—and are figuring out how to achieve it. Either that or they're discovering what they're passionate about, how they can change the world, and selecting a college or a life path to get there.

This is not to say that I wish girls were more like boys or that boys do not deal with their own toxic sets of values . . . but there could not *be* a worse time in life for girls or women to be duped into skipping their internal development. We're losing an enormous amount of time at a crucial juncture without realizing it. By the time it dawns on us that we don't know who we are, we're married or divorced or in the wrong job or city, and we're trapped.

So instead of undertaking the now-monumental task of figuring out who we really are and what that might mean, we curl our hair, take another selfie, slap some filters on it, and wait for the dopamine boost when strangers call us hot. If we look good enough online, then maybe everything really is OK.

As hard as women work, as far as we have come, we deserve better than that.

But then again, most of us can't afford to throw away our phones and swear off social media. Once we unplug from tech culture, it does not stop; it just leaves us behind, and all signs point to its acceleration. So what can we do? How can we resist the constant sucking out of our selves through our screens and onto our timelines?

It begins with the realization that privacy—interiority—is a valuable trait.

WELL ADJUSTED?

One of the more encouraging aspects of modernity is the realization that traditional scientific studies, when they include only straight white males as test subjects, may not be universally applicable. This is the case with the work of Carol Gilligan who, in 1982, proposed that mental health and developmental markers for women are different from those for men.

Instead of looking for traditional measures of psychological health proposed by other researchers in her field (such as a balance of the ego with others' needs and the ability to accomplish one's goals), Gilligan conducted exhaustive interviews with girls and women and found that, even when we are excelling at all the milestones considered essential for men, women are missing something. This was illustrated in *Meeting at the Crossroads*, her work with colleague Lyn Mikel Brown at the Laurel School, a highly selective girls' prep school in Ohio.

The girls whom Brown and Gilligan studied were excelling developmentally: they exhibited the ability to empathize, realized that there were viewpoints other than their own, could differentiate their own thoughts and feelings from those of others, and were strong academically—all of which would be considered signs of complete and healthy development in boys. But, said Brown and Gilligan, while these girls were excellent at understanding and adjusting to *others'* needs and feelings, their *own* self-knowledge was gradually disappearing. According to Stephanie Wellen Levine, a lecturer at Tufts University, "Their research subjects seemed to lack intangible but deeply important qualities like self-knowledge and psychological flexibility, and they often shrank back when conflicts developed to preserve the illusion of goodwill among everyone involved."[19] In other words, as these girls were integrating into society and learning to be functional adults, they were losing the ability to hear their own voices.

This strange contradiction was highlighted by Levine in her book *Mystics, Mavericks, and Merrymakers: An Intimate Journey Among Hasidic Girls*, about the Lubavitch (a subset of Hasidic Judaism) community in Crown Heights, Brooklyn. The Hasidic girls Levine studied, in contrast to the Laurel girls, had powerful senses of their inner selves: they were "forceful and proud, yet completely within the boundaries of Lubavitch expectations," displaying wicked senses of humor and brilliant intelligence, *especially* after puberty.[20] In fact, instead of muffling their uniqueness to avoid conflict, they prized their individuality.

By so-called traditional measures, these girls were undeveloped—according to Levine, "They are dependent on external authorities, both human and divine. They are aware of different cultures but from a seemingly closed-minded vantage point; they believe their system is unequivocally the best, and the only path toward the truth."[21] However,

> from ardent questioner to popular kid to brooding scholar, these young women have an exquisitely refined sense of their feelings and thoughts. They are open about their insights and willing to share them with a trusted outsider. Often, they handle intense conflict with poise, grit, self-understanding, and courage, whether they be questioners struggling with desires that flout Hasidic values or religious stalwarts aching for like-minded peers and a more pious community. In other words, when it comes to the strength, development, and expression of the psyche—an internal awareness of their ideas and feelings and an ability to share this knowledge with others—these young women thrive.[22]

Wow. These young ladies sound like the opposite of the hollowed-out girls mainstream culture seems to idolize and produce—and I'm including myself in that latter group, as demonstrated by my desire to undertake the Experiment. What makes these Hasidic girls so attuned to their inner selves?

TZNIUT

Hasidic Jews, like Amish people in Pennsylvania, are easy to spot because they dress so differently from the secular world. Often the men are in dark suits and hats, and the women wear long skirts and wigs or scarves. Also like the Amish, they are considered to be ultraobservant relative to other branches of Judaism. By now, it should be apparent that different communities in each faith tradition interpret the words of God in unique ways, and it's no different for the Jewish faith, the oldest of the three Abrahamic traditions. I was personally inspired by more Orthodox Jewish dress due to my exposure to it in Brooklyn, but Jewish modesty, called *tzniut*, is adhered to by religiously inclined Jewish folks across the spectrum of belief. It should also be apparent that an obsessive focus on dress as the only way to express modesty is not only unhelpful but also reductive. Modesty isn't just about the body and how much is revealed but also about behavior and values.

The framework for tzniut comes from two places: "the *dath Moshe*, or those requirements specified in the Torah itself, and the *dath Yehudith*, or generations of rabbinic interpretation and commentary that represent variations established through time and across space by different Jewish communities."[23] The requirements for tzniut for women in general are as follows: women cannot wear pants, since each gender must wear clothes made for his or her specified sex and pants are considered to be for men; women must cover the arms including the elbows, the legs including the knees, and the collarbone; and married women must cover the hair, with either a wig (*sheytl*) or a head scarf (*tikhl*). Some women wear both at the same time, because a woman's hair is considered an *ervah*—an erotic stimulus, like breasts or thighs—and must be completely hidden from all but the woman's husband.

The head-scarf-only look is generally associated with the women of the Satmar Hasidic community in the Brooklyn neighborhood of Williamsburg; the women I saw pushing strollers in my neighborhood were likely part of this subgroup.[24] Bright colors, such as red and orange, and patterns may also be considered improper, and tight clothing is also frowned upon. In some communities, in an effort to keep erotic stimulus to a minimum, women may not sing in the company of men.

What inspired me about tzniut as I was designing the Experiment was the reasoning behind it. Jewish women are taught from a very young age that their *neshama*—soul—is the most valuable part of them, and that they should guard it from outside corruption because it is precious. As far as I know, Christians are taught to value their souls too, but for many young Christian girls, the constant pressure to stay virginal and make promises to stay that way communicates the message that women's bodies—particularly our "purity"—are far more important than anything else about us. Our souls are often painted as important only when it comes to making sure they go to heaven after we die. This message, of course, is augmented by secular culture as it pushes women to be sexy but not sexual.

The purpose of tzniut, according to author Gila Manolson in her first book, *Outside/Inside: A Fresh Look at Tzniut*, is to "look good, but without flaunting yourself. It urges you to downplay your body in order to reveal your soul. This doesn't mean wearing shapeless, drab clothing. It means being attractive in a way that draws attention past your physicality to your personhood."[25] The aim is not to conceal what is shameful (the female body, supposedly) but to highlight what is precious (the soul). This is related to what I learned the first night I went out with friends: one does not have to be sloppy to be modest.

Of course, tzniut is not an example of pure feminist ideology that somehow stands in contrast to the misogyny embedded in an

Abrahamic religion, born in the antiwoman cultural cradle of the ancient Near East. There is an element in Jewish modesty of women bearing responsibility for "helping" men stay focused, because the poor things can't concentrate if we look too sexy. Manolson, who is a practicing Orthodox Jew (so modest, but not to the extent of Hasidic women), says, "Males, it has been observed, have trouble focusing on spiritual matters when around less than modestly clad females. . . . Women are indeed held responsible (within limits) for the effect their attire has upon men, just as all Jews are responsible for one another."[26] Urgh. There's that whole "love thy neighbor, cover up for him" reasoning again. Additionally, Orthodox and ultra-Orthodox women who do not conform to their communities' standards are sometimes shamed. Said one member of an Orthodox community of her experience with wigs versus scarves, "I mean, really, a Jewish woman's worst enemy is, well, another Jewish woman. I honestly feel that way. If you don't go along with the crowd, they try to make you an outcast."[27]

So, just because a woman is Jewish and modest does not mean she's free from the problematic aspects of body policing that so often show up both in secular culture and in religious traditions that have traditionally been patriarchal. Wendy Shalit, one of the best-known self-styled "modesty-niks" in Jewish feminist literature, consistently links modest clothing with sexual continence—in other words, dress modestly, stay virginal until marriage. She does make some of the same points I do: "The prevailing view is that if you think sexuality should be private or special, then you must be ashamed of it. You're a prude. Conversely, if you are 'comfortable with your sexuality,' then you should be 'cool' with lifting your shirt for strangers or cheering on your man as he enjoys a lap dance with another woman."[28] She questions the female chauvinist pig version of feminism (without using the term) and bemoans the linkage of women's liberation with women's ability to fool around with whomever we want. She connects the objectification of young girls with their increased promiscuity and explains that we're losing something vital by having multiple sexual partners.

I respect Shalit's commitment to her religious beliefs, but it's time to stop linking how women dress with what we do in the bedroom. I think it's another way to codify male ownership of women, when the reality is that what we do with our bodies does not need to be explained, by either our modes of dress or our words, to the people around us. It's just not anyone else's business, and we don't owe anyone information about our private selves. By continuing to draw connections between how women dress and our supposed sex lives, we're reinforcing the exteriority rather than the interiority of women. Besides, there is no real link for today's young women between what they wear and their sexual behavior: even young girls are expected to look sexy but not to engage in actual sexual activity lest they be branded sluts.

Though I am, again, not advocating that women behave like men—we are very different, and I like it that way—think of how no one expects a man's clothing to connote his sex life. Perhaps if he's in a thong in a Pride parade we assume he's gay, but if he's in a flannel top, do women get to walk up to him and, if he won't respond to our advances, get angry because his shirt implies that he's willing to perform oral sex on us? What if he wears skinny jeans? When he sits down next to us on the bus, do we make a pass at him, assuming that since his pants are tight he *wants* us to hit on him, and then throw a fit when he puts on headphones? If he's in a suit, do we assume that no matter what he says ("I'm married," "I don't like you," "You're my boss") he desires intercourse? We have no idea, looking at a man, who he is in the privacy of the bedroom, and no one demands to know what his sex life is like by forcing him to wear a costume that supposedly tells us about it.

Some insist that men are visual creatures, and so they somehow need the world to tell them who's available. But if the tables were turned—if men had to walk around all day showing their shoulders and in butt-hugging pants—I would be distracted too. Seeing other people in very little clothing is distracting to anyone, and there's nothing "natural" about one gender being expected to cater to the other gender by advertising their most private selves. Again, it's just a costume. Men are allowed to decouple how they dress from their most intimate selves because they are allowed to be more than their bodies. They are expected to fulfill a different, and perhaps equally restrictive, set of expectations, but these expectations are tied to what they *do*, not how they *look*. If women believe ourselves to be more than bodies, we should stop highlighting our physicality, simply because it's more in line with how we see ourselves—as people, not things.

If all women were taught, as the Lubavitch girls are, that we have a natural connection to the universe and we already know what our truth is, *and that that knowledge is sufficient to govern our own lives and bodies,* how receptive would we be to men telling us we're being prudes because we won't send nudes or we don't respond with unrestrained joy to his unsolicited dick pic? Would we wheedle and apologize and eventually cave like we're taught to do, or would we tell him to fuck off, block his number, and not lose sleep? Alisa, an Orthodox convert who is working toward a law degree, said, "There is no doubt that what I love about it [Orthodoxy] is the way in which women are understood....We are the holders of the key for the most important aspect of inner life. The experience of being a woman in Judaism I would say is like Jungian 'anima'—a profound introspection and inner intensity."[29] It is this self-value and interiority that undergirds tzniut, and I find it inspiring.

FREEDOM

The self-assured young women in the Lubavitch community from *Mystics, Mavericks, and Merrymakers* lead very different lives than most secular girls. They are prohibited from any interaction with males to whom they are not related, attending a separate school from the boys, socializing only with other girls, and generally living in an all-female world except at home. They wear long skirts and opaque tights, long sleeves with denim skirts, and often, sneakers. Until they are married, Lubavitch girls do not cover their hair. These are all interpretations of tzniut upheld by the community, though of course some girls push the boundaries, wearing skirts that are a little too tight or too short or wearing high socks in hot weather instead of tights.

How these girls dress is not the only differentiating factor, then, between the Hasidic girls and women like me. But the reason they dress the way they do is an expression of the way they think of themselves, encapsulated in a biblical verse that is very different from the Christian verses traditionally used to support modesty. Levine explains, "The idea of tznius derives from this verse from the Psalms:'The entire glory of the daughter of the king lies on the inside.'[30] Within an Orthodox Jewish scheme, this concept is not at all pejorative; true holiness is by nature private."[31] There's that core concept, the one women might do well to remember amid the tech revolution: the importance of privacy. The beauty of interiority. The idea that the most valuable thing about women is our voices, not our objecthood.

Sometimes, though, those voices rise up against the traditions that cultivated them, and women who attempt to leave these safe enclaves suffer. When they realize that they cannot be both themselves and members of their religion, the women who leave their conservative backgrounds must struggle mightily. The internal voices they've been encouraged to heed are apparently not supposed to say certain things.

Leah Vincent, a rabbi's daughter in the ultra-Orthodox Yeshivish community in Pittsburgh, regularly sat through dinner conversations in which the patriarch confidently proclaimed things like "A woman's brain cannot handle Talmud."[32] Taught that "College was a distraction, an invitation to a corrupt world that would only belittle a woman and seduce a man," and that "God is sickened by your bare legs,"[33] Leah can't handle the brutal expulsion from her observant family that begins with her writing notes to her crush and escalates when she wears an "immodest" sweater. She moves to New York, attempts suicide; her life falls apart, and with each painful incident her parents push her further and further away, claiming that she is disappointing them. She eventually "goes *frei*"—free—but she does a lot of damage to herself in the process, damage that stems in part from being brought up to believe that "modesty was a girl's most important mission" and all that such a reductive gender role implies.[34]

Leah Lax, a former member of the Hasidic community in Dallas who chronicled her experiences in *Uncovered: How I Left Hasidic Life and Finally Came Home*, found that there was no room in Hasidism for her, in part because she is a lesbian. Once she realized that she could not be happy in her Orthodox life, there was no other alternative than to divorce her husband and exit the community. She has a particularly jarring realization while helping an artist friend with a combination photo-and-story exhibit called *The Mikvah Project* (a *mikvah* being the sacred pool Orthodox women immerse themselves in for ritual purification). An Orthodox interviewee, Dinah, erases the messiness of her past, with which Leah is intimately familiar, in favor of a sanitized version of how she came to Hasidism, and Leah is outraged at the falseness of her narrative. When she arrives at home after the interview, Leah rips her wig off and throws it down the hallway: "In our wigs, Dinah and I are identical members of the same faceless ranks."[35]

So it's not fair to say that tzniut, with its emphasis on interiority, is the magic pill, the antidote to the hollowing-out of women's souls through tech. In the known history of the Western world, women have never had as many freedoms as we do now, and many of us have never been so committed to equality; we have also never had access to a digital space that is simultaneously unreal and more real than life itself.

Can tzniut inspire us to blaze a completely new trail, one more in step with the new, ever-broadening world in which women find ourselves?

A BETTER YARDSTICK

Traditional markers of healthy development—awareness of others' viewpoints, empathy, and independence from authority figures like parents and teachers—are appropriate for men who want to become well-rounded human beings. Males in Western culture are taught to be self-reliant and excel regardless of the cost, so they need empathy and humility to make them balanced adults.

But for women, others' needs are not where we need work. We *know* how to empathize, how to get out of the way for others. The problem is that we're told to self-silence and self-objectify, and by the time we're adults we feel as though we have no selves at all. Rather than making us functional adults with healthy boundaries and views, this makes us dependent children who constantly need direction and approval, who cannot navigate conflict, and who are overdependent on others to define them.

Western culture is at a turning point where many realize that if half of us are expected to be puppets, no one will be happy—and even if some *are* unhappy with this new world, that kind of doesn't matter. Women are tired of having to be nonbeings just to avoid making others uncomfortable, constantly cleaning up and shrinking and attending to fragile egos. Collectively we can't do it anymore, and we shouldn't have to. To blossom, women need a way to protect our innermost selves and assert our boundaries, skills that online culture actively inhibits.

I once had a voice teacher who told me something that changed my life. Learning to sing is essentially learning to get out of the way of the vocal cords so they can be free and expressive, but paradoxically, when singers open our mouths, the first thing we try to do is make our voices sound different. Voice lessons are really just learning to let your voice be what it already is.

In order to do this, my teacher told me, "it doesn't help you to think, 'Don't do that.' Because if you're not doing 'that,' what are you doing? You can't do nothing; if you're doing nothing, then you're not singing. So rather than telling yourself not to do 'that,' you have to tell yourself, 'Do this.' *Then*, the voice can be free." It was the difference between negative and positive reinforcement, between scolding myself when I messed up and concentrating on what I wanted instead.

So if women don't self-objectify online . . . what *do* we do?

ATLANTA, LATE JUNE 2011

www.okcupid.com

I have some notifications. *Ooh. New messages.*

From zenromantic: "You have passed my rigorous entrance exam. You may talk to my Dad. Mazel tov!"

I blink at the screen. *Well. This is new.*

After trying the traditional way to meet people to date (talking to them in person), I have decided I am tired of explaining the Experiment. I joke that I should just carry around a PowerPoint with me; I am so sick of telling people why I both cover my hair *and* swear like a sailor. Instead, I explain myself via profile and hope that whoever contacts me has read that, yes, I am in seminary, and no, I am not antievolution. Yes, I am a feminist; no, I do not hate men. Yes, I dress modestly; no, I am not a virgin.

Which has led to this cute but confusing message from what looks from the profile picture like a huge black guy with multi-colored hair. Well, more accurately, from his thirteen-year-old daughter.

In the coming months I will find out that on the way to school in the morning, she reads him profiles from OkCupid, which she made him sign up for after his divorce. If she gets all the way to the end of the profile without him saying, "Ew" or "Nope," she emails the woman. Hence, the entrance-exam comment. (I wish I could explain why she used *mazel tov*, though. Neither of them is Jewish.) He knows I am a progressive religious feminist, but he has not even seen my face when she emails me.

We've been messaging for weeks, not yet meeting up, when he throws a party at his house. He invites me: it would be a good way to meet, without any pressure.

He is downstairs playing the bass in the garage band he heads up. I am upstairs when another guest turns on HBO's *Real Sex* in the background, and I watch forlornly as women spin around poles in thongs and talk about how empowering it is. I mutter something about, "Oh, not this bullshit again."

"What was that?" says a voice behind me.

I turn around, and it's the guy from OkCupid—Less. He's staring down at me with interest. Not sexual interest; he actually wants to know what I've said.

I am stone-cold sober, but before I can moderate my response, my voice comes pouring out of me: no high, wheedling "please like me" whine; no question marks at the ends of sentences; all opinion and perspective and, yeah, self-righteousness; and no, I am not smiling or trying, at all, to make sure he's comfortable. I think I finish with "I'm just tired of being told that the best way for me to be empowered is to take my clothes off."

He doesn't laugh. He doesn't look scared or confused (or bored). Instead, he sits down on the staircase. After a second, he says, "Well, but that's not the only way to be empowered. Is it?"

If he said anything at all about this, I was expecting, "Ha, ha. Tell me how you *really* feel!" or, "Hey, who are you to tell those women how to express their sexuality?" Instead, he actually states his opinion, *and then he asks me what I think.* When he talks with me he wants to know what I believe, not how to make me like him. I have never, in my life, been reacted to this way by a man.

I blink at him. *Who* is *this guy?*

I've struggled for five years about whether to include the above story, because for fuck's sake, the Modesty Experiment did not need to be validated by a man coming in and sweeping me off my feet.

But he didn't. He sort of showed up and walked next to me while I swept myself off my feet. And I can't help it if people reduce my work to "Feminist dresses modestly, meets man of her dreams, settles down." Because if there's one thing I learned from the *Salon* debacle, it's that no matter what you say, people will misinterpret your words. That doesn't mean you should shut up.

I decided to tell the truth about my husband's arrival in my life during the Experiment at this point in the story because it shows that technology doesn't *have* to be a Digital Suit. In fact, the only way I could get people to understand who I was, under the head scarf, was to either expend an enormous amount of energy repeating myself or write it out online. This was because the baggage about how I looked—modest—carried the opposite set of assumptions, for most people I encountered, about who I was underneath. In my case, my *online presence* was telling the truth about me; it was the *cultural interpretation* of modest dress that was a lie.

And yes, I received ignorant messages on OkCupid from guys wanting to explain to me why what I was doing was wrong and how they actually understood religion or feminism better than I did, despite simply being dudes with a passing interest in said topics, and would I like to get a drink so "we" (read: he) could talk about it? But no matter what women do, online or in real life, we get that kind of response. In 2011, there wasn't a word for it, but now it's called mansplaining.

Here's something odd: it actually felt good to be told I was wrong for standing up for something instead of being told I was wrong just for *being* (too fat, ugly, a prude, a tease, and so on). Somehow, putting who I really was out there, and being yelled at for that, was easier than trying to put a perfect self out there and still not being good enough.

Whether we like it or not, modest dress is tied to restrictive gender roles, and as of today, the exposed women are still considered the enlightened ones. But the online world offers women a new frontier. We can use it to fortify the idea that only women who conform to narrow beauty standards and who self-objectify are worthy of the label "empowered," or we can tell the truth about ourselves and see what happens.

This is a tall and perhaps unrealistic order in a world where anonymity supports meanness (and dick pics). I am not asking women to bare our souls on the internet—I don't even think that's a particularly good idea for some of us. But what would happen if every time we put something online, we asked ourselves, "Who is this for? Do I want validation that the image I've put out is sufficiently impressive? Or do I want to clarify who I really am to others? And if it's the second one, is the exposure worth it *to me*?"

I can tell you from personal experience, it might be worth it, but only if you choose it freely. I'm glad I met my husband online and I would not have if I hadn't been so honest in my profile . . . but the comments on the blog I ran and the Facebook page I have about the Experiment sometimes make me want to claw my eyes out.

One of the best things about the internet, though, is that it makes available the ideas of those one would never encounter in real life. To be more specific, feminism has a louder voice because brave women get online, every day, and fight the Twitter trolls and write articles and explain, yet again, why telling us to smile is not the innocuous gesture men are trained to believe it is. When our friends say sexist stuff online, we can send them links to articles, rather than having to sit down with them and expend yet more psychological energy on living in a world where emotional labor is women's work. (If we're at the stage of having to send them articles, they probably aren't the kind of people who'll read such articles anyway. But at least they can't claim they don't have access to the information.)

Or, maybe interiority means something more extreme: What would happen if women were simply more intentional about valuing our private selves *over* our curated online ones? What would happen if we limited the time we spent online as a feminist act? Could we train ourselves to stop self-objectifying and learn other ways to self-soothe? Could we learn to notice when we're walking through the park thinking, "I have to tweet about this," and then think, "No," and reach out and touch the grass instead, *because our lives are not products to be consumed*?

Recrafting our relationships with the Digital Suit won't work if we just yell at ourselves not to cultivate them. Like my voice teacher said, we have to tell ourselves what *to* do instead. And I wish I could make some sort of blanket statement about what women *should* try when we get that itch to post on Facebook for likes ("Drink tea!" "Count to ten!"). That dopamine rush we get from the approval of others is potent, and sometimes we crave it without even realizing it's what we want. But the whole point here is that women need to learn our internal landscapes, what makes us feel grounded. That's going to be different for everyone, so any prescription I could make would be pointless.

Obviously, online attention feels good. And an internet presence is necessary socially and professionally, and that's not likely to change. But there's got to be a way to engage with the ever-expanding world of technology that doesn't just saddle women with another Suit, another set of expectations to satisfy, another way to make life more fun for dudes while our own precious time disappears down the drain.

The human brain is nothing if not plastic. We *can* learn.

CHAPTER SIX

WORLDWIDE BEAUTY

The "Social Skin"

ATLANTA, SEPTEMBER 2011

I have been sitting in this chair for fourteen hours. I remembered that pain and beauty often went hand in hand, but this is silly.

For the end of the Experiment, because I'm treating myself, I've decided to go to the same place Less, my then-boyfriend and future husband, gets his locks, and get some myself. (I have since decided to stay away from dreadlocks due to the discomfort many black folks feel about white people wearing them. It took the internet's influence to remind me that though Less did not have a problem with locks on white folks, Less does not represent all black people everywhere.) But right after the Experiment I want long hair again, and this is the best way to get it. When Heather, my hairdresser, is done, I have a head of long, twisted fibers in reddish-blond and purple. I look fabulous.

A few days later, on the night of my thirtieth birthday party, I wear a strapless dress. It feels weird. I also have to "do" my makeup—meaning, wear more than the concealer and mascara I wore when I preached—for the first time in nine months. I haven't forgotten how or anything, but putting on eyeshadow, matching the colors and everything, is both fun and slightly strange to me. Am I worse at it? I'm not sure.

I have a great night with my friends, even though most don't show up: my boyfriend's house is "outside the perimeter," which in Atlanta-speak means far away. I don't feel super exposed, but I'm aware, again, of how much I must think about how I look at all times—whether my eyeliner is smudging, how I'm standing, whether I need to reapply my lipstick. After a few hours, I change into jeans and a T-shirt and feel immediately at ease.

With some neighbors, Less and I end the night on the candlelit back porch with a guitar, singing as the frogs in the pond behind the house cheep away. All in all, turning thirty feels like bursting into bloom rather than falling off the tree.

I'd learned a lot in the nine months of the Experiment. I'd learned how powerful the Suit was, for marking identity and signaling to others who I was, and what happened when I took it off. But one thing I couldn't get beyond was the influence of my own culture on my sphere of options. Did women in other countries have to wear a costume that assured men of their primary place in society, or was that just a US thing? Were there universally sexy body parts, like hair or shoulders?

No, of course not. The way women are expected to behave, to perform femininity, is different all over the world and is shaped by the history, religion, and values of the particular culture. Seen through this lens, the way women in the US are expected to conform to beauty standards seems just as arbitrary—as indeed it is—as any other set of mores. The more we know about these other options, the looser the hold of the Suit on our own lives. Adherence to the rules of the Suit becomes less of an imperative and more of a language.

I find this to be a very reassuring thought.

WEALTH IN CLOTH: AFRICA

Though it's impossible to accurately generalize customs on a continent as large as Africa, it's often suggested, by writers who live or have spent time there, that cloth—the cloth itself and also how it is worn—is a way of communicating status and dignity, as well as a form of social and even material currency. In other words, female power is communicated by more, not less, clothing. The emphasis, broadly speaking, is not on "sexiness" or youth as it is in the States, but on the ability of a woman to present herself with style, in outfits that are well put together, current, and worn in the most becoming way. Status is still communicated by clothing, but the emphasis on the male gaze as a lodestar is, by and large, missing; "dress competence" is emphasized over sex appeal.

For example, the women of Lomé, Togo's capital, are "renowned throughout the coast of Guinea and beyond" for their ability to dress well, says anthropologist Nina Sylvanus.[1] Many of the women of West Africa wear *pagne*, a type of colorful cloth that can be used for everything from wrapped skirts to head wraps to tailored outfits, and often the skirt and head wrap are made from the same pattern. The quality and cost of a woman's pagne are powerful indicators of her social status, and viewers can tell at a glance what a woman's place in society is just by looking at whether the pagne is an original of Dutch origin or a Chinese copy, whether the pattern it bears is in the latest style, and so forth.

This is part of Africa's "historical concern with body decoration as a sign of status. . . . Unlike the Victorian ideals of idealized femininity and middle-class domesticity that became a symbol of [European] national culture, respectable femininity in Togo was less concerned with modesty and discretion than it was with dress competence, power, and taste. Respectable femininity was evaluated by means of a woman's fashionability."[2] In other words, if a Togolese woman wants respect, the best way to communicate this expectation is for her to dress immaculately.

This notion that social regard is marked by sartorial elegance is one found throughout Africa. For the Kalabari, a tribe that inhabits the western Niger Delta region of Nigeria, how to attire oneself—from the way to tie a head wrap to the selection of appropriate accessories—is the subject of frequent household discussion, and when women must dress very formally, elder female relatives are summoned to select and style ensembles. Each member represents the family, lineage, and even ancestors of the community, and so before anyone goes out, one is appraised by one's kin, adding the implication that if one is not dressed well, one does not enjoy the luxury of a family that cares about that person.

The eldest female is the guardian of a cloth box, which is the chest of ancestral clothing that is opened and used on special occasions. According to one source, "Artistry in dress is determined not only by the contents of the cloth boxes but access to them; as guardian of the family cloth boxes and dispenser of their contents, the eldest female controls the male lineage property and its use."[3] This cloth, passed down from generation to generation, is a way of communicating status and of honoring one's ancestors, and the more storied the cloth, the higher the respect it commands.

Elsewhere in Nigeria, the concept of wealth in cloth bolsters a woman's social regard and can even influence her political standing. Anthropologist Misty L. Bastain, who did her field research in Nigeria, tells the story of Nwanneka. An Igbo woman who sought to claim the title of Omu Onicha, queen of Onitcha, in the late 1980s, Nwanneka appeared at various public events in carefully assembled outfits, bearing tasteful gifts, making herself visible as a candidate for the position.[4] According to Bastain, "Women's wealth in Igbo-speaking areas has historically been encoded in lavish displays of cloth and jewelry. Clean, rich, and eye-catching dress helped prove a woman's worth. If a woman emerged unkempt from her house, she was likely to be treated with disdain. . . . Away from home, a woman pursuing public stature must wear striking clothing while observing local norms of modesty and restraint."[5]

Since dressing well communicates dignity, it is not surprising that many residents of African countries have dealt with economic adversity by refusing to yield their stylish exteriors. (As a side note: this reminds me of something Heather, the lady who gave me my locks, told me when I asked her about whether she'd experienced any negative effects of the recession. She explained that she and her colleagues in the beauty business were actually doing *better*. She explained, "People will set aside money for this kind of stuff, because it makes them feel like they're OK.")

Sylvanus also mentions the economic realities of modern Togo in a way that sounds familiar to millennials in the US: "At a moment when university degrees and other recognized forms of qualifications have lost their value, the body itself becomes a valuable site of production for generating social capital that can potentially lead to unexpected employment opportunities."[6] Like YouTube videos leading to endorsement deals, perhaps, or getting Instagram famous?

In Zambia, the public debate about women's bodies—especially how much of them it is "decent" to expose—sounds strangely similar to that of the West. When the miniskirt came onto the international fashion scene in the 1960s and '70s, the response from established power structures was repressive, says Karen Tranberg Hansen, professor of anthropology emerita at Northwestern University. In 1971, the House of Chiefs passed a motion condemning women's skirts above the knee, trotting out the standard talking points of sumptuary police the world over: that when men see female flesh they are "naturally" aroused, that such exposure constituted an assault on "traditional" values, and that women who chose to dress in this way were corroding the fabric of society.[7] (Truly traditional Zambian clothing consisted of "bark cloth and animal hides" and exposed far more of women's bodies that miniskirts ever did.[8])

The same arguments took on a more sinister tone when miniskirts appeared again in the 1990s: women who wore them were publicly stripped in marketplaces—as in, had their clothes torn off—by gangs of young men who claimed they were "naturally" curious about the victim's body because she partially showed it to them. In this way, young women received the message that their safety and their clothing were inextricably linked, much the same way modern American women do.

It's interesting that this theme—when a woman wears less, she can't be surprised if men mistreat her—surfaces in such disparate cultures. It suggests that, indeed, when men see flesh they're liable to misbehave. But if that's true, how is taking off our clothing *empowering* for women? I know I am veering dangerously close to blaming women for the actions of men, so let me say instead: since men assault women all over the world and almost universally blame women, the conclusion seems to be that some men are just dangerous, no matter what women are wearing. Perhaps self-defense skills and boundary enforcement, not shame about how we look, should be a component of how female gender identity is conceptualized. After all, so many men are "just naturally curious."

NOMADS: NONMETROPOLITAN AFRICA

Not all Africans reside in cities, of course. But the encroaching influence of capitalist culture can be felt even in rural tribal life. For the Bedouin of North Africa, the culture clash between the norms of centralized, capitalist societies and those of nomadic tribal groups bears itself out in complex ways. The Bedouins are peoples descended from and identifying with the wandering societies who lived in the desert of North Africa and the Middle East, outside cities and towns; most identify as both Arabs and Muslims. They are generally a self-contained subgroup, traditionally earning their livelihood by herding. Divided into clans, their culture has been a bit of a closed system. Until the middle of the twentieth century, most Bedouins lived in tents and migrated with their herds, according to weather, grazing patterns, and other livestock-related concerns.

The typical Bedouin household contains a married couple plus their siblings or parents and children; work is divided up equally. The women make and maintain the tents and the households while the men tend to the herds. Bedouin society is patriarchal; it is also a society in which divorce is common. Bedouin women cover outside the home and do not show their hair or, often, their faces to men to whom they are not immediately related.[9]

However, non-Bedouin culture is encroaching. As the Egyptian state tries to integrate the Bedouin, the Awlad 'Ali tribe has settled into more permanent communities that are connected by commerce with the wider Egyptian economy. As a result, the Bedouin have consistent access to mass-produced goods. According to anthropologist Lila V. Abu-Lughod, this new lifestyle in which men are the breadwinners and these goods come to women only through their husbands alters the way young women see their role in Bedouin society. Young women in particular see consumerism and more Westernized ideals of marriage—that is, ones based on compatibility and more focused upon the individual woman's attractiveness, as opposed to the kinship ties between the bride's and groom's families—as stages for acts of resistance.

For example, in the 1980s, young Bedouin women began buying negligees for their wedding trousseaus. According to Abu-Lughod, "What the older women object to in the purchase of lingerie is not just the waste of precious money on useless items, but the immodesty of these emergent technologies of sexualized femininity to be deployed in the pleasing of husbands. . . . Members of this older generation at least as I saw them, were often dignified in comportment, but at the same time they were usually loud, sure of themselves, and hardly what we would consider feminine."[10] The older generation of Bedouin women were used to gaining familial rights and respect through their work and contributions to their kinsmen; the younger generation set their sights on gaining these things by pleasing their husbands, a shift ushered in by increased access to consumer culture.

It's interesting that male primacy, as reinforced by men's sole access to work and therefore money, has made its way into an ancient nomadic tribe in the space of only one generation, simply by proximity to consumer culture. It's also interesting how the young women of the tribe began to see their value more as man pleasers than as contributors to society. Today, young Bedouin women still wear veils, which are getting sheerer and sheerer, but women are still unable to work outside the home.

THE TRIBE OF THE VEILED MEN: THE TUAREG

Somewhat south of the Bedouin villages, another nomadic group can be found, also Muslim, in which veiling is interpreted in a singular way: the *men* veil, while the women do *not*. The Tuareg, who roam the Sahara Desert and whose roots are contested (some have blue or green eyes, leading historians to hypothesize about Jewish or even Viking roots[11]), consist of six or seven large confederations, each of which is made up of smaller clans. Known for their poetry and called by European explorers "the blue men of the desert" (the expensive indigo dye on their clothing bled onto their skin), the Tuareg are matrilineal. They are not *matriarchal*: the men make the political decisions. However, as the heads of the family, Tuareg women enjoy a surprising amount of freedom and respect, more than most Western women did at the start of the twentieth century.[12]

Tuareg men and women are considered to be equals, though they do not share space or eat together. Before marriage, young Tuareg women are allowed to have as many "boyfriends" as they like. According to one source, if a young man wishes to visit a young woman, he must do so "in the dead of night—totally silently, from the side and not the entrance, and remembering that his lover's mother and siblings sleep there too, but the couple may amuse themselves however they like, for as long as they like, so long as the young man creeps away, equally silently, before dawn. . . . The next night, if she likes, the girl may entertain herself with another boy."[13] Upon marriage, a woman receives a dowry, usually a tent, from her mother, along with livestock, and the man moves into his new wife's family's encampment. Upon divorce—which is common and considered normal—the wife retains all property. Tuareg men expect to have at least two wives over the course of their lifetimes.

The origin of veiling among the Tuareg is mysterious. The men have pieces of cloth that they draw across their faces in the presence of women, particularly those they respect, such as a mother-in-law, strangers, and higher-status men; the greater the respect shown for the other party, the higher upon the nose the veil is worn. The highest-status male, if among men, does not need to cover his face. As with other Muslim societies, the veil is only removed in the presence of one's immediate family.

Again, the why of Tuareg veiling is unknown. But it is interesting to note that in an ancient society in which women are highly respected—one common saying among Tuareg men is "Everything comes to you from your mother"[14]—women are *not* expected to cover their faces. It makes one consider the point made earlier about how religion, in this case Islam, is interpreted to fit the surrounding culture and not the other way around. Said another way, if Islam were inherently oppressive toward women, the Tuareg would not proudly declare their love for Allah. It all depends, one might say, on who's reading the book.

SARIS AND CROCS: INDIA

Arshie Qureshi, the Kashmir-based reporter for the online magazine and platform *Feminism in India*, tells the story of being refused one of the "women's seats" (the first eight seats on buses in Kashmir) because she was dressed in jeans. When she boarded the bus, she noticed that there was nowhere for her to sit and, seeking to make a point, attempted to take a picture of the men seated under the Women Only sign. When she did, a man stood up and shouted at her that she should "dress as a lady first," meaning, explains Qureshi, that she should be wearing a *salwar kameez* (what's currently considered traditional dress in Kashmir) in order to enjoy the provisions specifically set aside for women. Predictably, the other passengers on the bus pretended to ignore the whole affair. The same man later offered his seat to a woman in hijab, talking with her and laughing loudly enough for Qureshi to hear about "seat activists."[15]

In many ways, Indian women enjoy far less liberty than those of other countries. Geetanjali Gangoli of the University of Bristol explains that, as of 2007, "only one in three women can go to the market without permission from their family, and one in four visit friends and relatives without permission. . . . The average age for marriage for women in India is 12.6."[16] Indian law has roughly the same prohibitions against discrimination as that of the US. Gangoli says the penal codes, include Article 14, which guarantees the right to equal protection under the law; Article 15, which forbids discrimination on the basis of religion, race, caste, sex, and place of birth; Article 25, which guarantees freedom of religion; and Article 29, which guarantees to minorities "the right to conserve their culture."[17]

The art of blending what's seen as "traditional" Indian dress with modern options is one that Indian women are expected to master. (I put the word "traditional" in quotes because, according to many scholars, the concept of what is traditionally Indian is influenced quite a bit by British, Muslim, and miscellaneous fashion and cultural norms. As in Zambia and elsewhere, the concept of tradition is often a tool used to shame women into wearing more conservative clothing rather than a concept based on what is authentically traditional.)[18] The *New York Times* profiles Poornima Vardhan, an investment banker turned fashion professional who found she had to expand her wardrobe considerably when she moved from New York back to her native Delhi. The article explains that "India, unlike most other emerging countries, has managed to retain its clothing traditions even among the upper classes. Although bluejeans are now popular here [Delhi], their sales are still dwarfed by those of saris."[19]

With regard to modesty, a woman is expected to expertly navigate the lines between traditional dress and frumpiness, attractiveness and showing too much. The *Times* went on:

Modesty is a crucial part of the adjustment to India. While the country has none of the strict clothing laws of some avowedly Muslim nations, a woman's knees are rarely displayed. A group of Muslim clerics in Kashmir recently demanded that female tourists refrain from wearing shorts. In Delhi, few weeks pass without some report of a woman being gang-raped, and even some prominent Indian women blame the victims if they happen to have been wearing clothing deemed immodest.[20]

The article also quotes Mukulika Banerjee of the London School of Economics and Political Science:"A complete no-no in Indian modesty is to show legs. . . . Cleavage is fine but not legs."[21] Bellies are also fine; in fact, travel blogger Rachel Jones claims, "That belly of yours? It can be shown to anyone! I see 100 Indian bellies every day in every city in India. Fat ones, skinny ones, in between. Doesn't matter; they're showing them off!"[22]

Again, regional differences make it impossible to outline hard-and-fast rules for how Indian women are expected to dress. But it is interesting to note that despite its well-documented problems with violence against women, India twice elected Indira Gandhi as prime minister; she served from 1966 to 1977, and again from 1980 until her assassination in 1984. Though the election of a member of an underrepresented group to the highest public office does not signal the end of prejudice against that group—the Obama administration, for example—one wonders how national support for a female prime minister was achieved in a country where women are so egregiously discriminated against. Contrast this with the United States, where women are ostensibly so much more liberated, and yet Americans would still rather elect a man with no experience, preparation, or talent for the office of president than see a woman in such a position.

"OOH, ASIAN PERSUASION": JAPAN AND CHINA

In the United States, Asian women are often stereotyped as the sexiest, being light skinned, thin, and supposedly naturally docile. But what about Asian women in the Asian cultures I haven't covered yet? For example, how do Japanese or Chinese women understand and respond to the expectations about femininity placed on them by their respective cultures?

Like India, Japan has a rich sartorial history that is currently intersecting with and influencing Western fashion. Unlike India, however, in Japan, Western clothing is generally worn every day, and traditional dress, such as the kimono, is reserved for special or ceremonial occasions. Though Japanese women have had their own feminist revolutions, cultural concepts such as the "Christmas cake," a term that refers to women over twenty-five as being past the age of marriage desirability, are just now beginning to fall away.[23] Gender differences are evident in spoken Japanese, in which women are expected to use softer, gentler words than men, and men are expected to be "ideal workers" while women are still primarily responsible for what happens inside the home.[24]

As Western feminism resurfaced in the 1960s, a simultaneous movement was evolving in Japan. Mitsu Tanaka wrote her 1970 manifesto "Liberation from the Toilet" (Tanaka used the word "toilet" because women at the time were denigrated as either mothers or merely repositories for men's bodily fluids[25]) to express her outrage at being disallowed from being herself, because, she explained, she was too busy being forced to fit into the narrow, male-defined box of "woman." While Western feminists were protesting the Miss America pageant, Japanese feminism had a different emphasis. In response to American feminists' focus on the trappings of beauty as oppression, Tanaka says, in an article in the *Japan Times*, "It's never black or white. Sometimes you might want to wear makeup, other days you might not. We were ordinary women just trying to live our lives truthfully."[26]

Westerners may also think of a strange kind of cuteness that pervades much of Japanese dress, with Hello Kitty's adorable face gracing backpacks and the huge, glazed eyes of manga characters staring out at us from magazines and bookshelves. Something quietly rebellious is happening within these seemingly infantilizing trends. Japanese cultural studies scholar Masafumi Monden argues that this cuteness—called *kawaii*—constitutes a remaking of female cultural space. In fact, says Monden, this "amalgamation of 'asexual' cuteness and girlish reinvention of 'authenticity' can serve as an alternative to the established multiple binaries of aggression, sexualization and modesty in which women tend to be represented."[27] In other words Japanese adults, particularly women, can choose to be cute and pretty without automatic sexualization.

Monden generally defines *kawaii* as "an aesthetic that celebrates sweet, adorable, simple, infantile, delicate and pretty visual, physical or behavioural qualities"[28] and explains that it can include girls *and* boys. Pinafores, knee socks, ribbons, and flowers can all be used, perhaps surprising for European American audiences, to subvert expectations that adult women must always be ready to respond to the sexual desires of men. Instead, kawaii provides an opportunity to look feminine without automatically being objectified. This may seem weird to Western audiences, but perhaps this is because we are mostly incapable of seeing adult women without applying our standards of sexual desirability. American culture in particular is known for forcing objectification upon younger and younger females (think of the sexually suggestive clothes of Bratz dolls), but the assumption that female means sex simply isn't there in the Japanese mind, says Monden. Quoting Merry White's *Material Child: Coming of Age in Japan and America*, Monden says that for the Japanese, "'Giving off the scent' of sexuality is publicly frowned upon."[29]

This is not to say that Japan is a wonderland of autonomy and freedom for women. The *Economist*'s "Glass Ceiling Index," which grades the twenty-six wealthiest countries and compiles data on where women's work lives might be best, found that as of 2013 Japan and South Korea were the two worst countries in the world for working women.[30] Sexual assault is grossly underreported in Japan: only 4 percent of sexual assault victims notify authorities, and of those, more than half the cases are dropped.[31] (Compare this to the still shockingly low rates in the US, where one in three rapes is ever reported to the police, and only six rapists in one thousand will ever see the inside of a jail cell.)[32] Japanese women have their own struggles related to their safety and autonomy, but *kawaii* culture is, contrary to what it may look like to Western viewers, an assertion of autonomy in the sweetest of disguises.

In the People's Republic of China, where the Cultural Revolution ostensibly sought to make men and women equal (so that they could work equally), the ancient roots of Confucian patriarchy still make their influence felt. Traditionally, women were expected to submit to male authority for the entirety of their lives: "a woman must obey her father before marriage, her husband after marriage, and her son after the death of the husband."[33] According to Confucian philosophy, the woman's place was inside the home, and the man's, outside—which, of course, broke down to the same gender roles seen elsewhere today, with the woman being responsible for domestic life, and the man being expected to provide for his family with paid employment outside the home.[34]

Today, with the increasing influence of cosmopolitanism, women are no longer expected to stay at home. However, says Xinyan Jiang, professor of philosophy at the University of Redlands,

> in current China, women are not appreciated and respected as much as men by employers, family members, and communities. Female infants are not welcome in many rural families; many more girls drop out of school than boys because many families value boys' education more than girls'; female workers are usually laid off before their male coworkers; female college or graduate school students have a much harder time getting good jobs than do their male classmates.[35]

So, though women are working outside the home and even excelling in male-dominated fields like aerospace engineering, their contributions still are not as highly valued as those of men.[36] Much like in the US.

The stereotypes about the way Chinese women dress, either as uniformed Iron Girls of the Communist state or submissive, sexualized ladies in *qipao* (the traditional Chinese silk dresses with the formfitting lines, short sleeves, and high collars, which are now seen primarily in the service industry), are artifacts of China's tumultuous sociopolitical history. In the aftermath of the homogenizing force of Mao's rule, in which deviation, even in physical appearance, was punished, modern Chinese femininity is in a "state of flux," says Sally E. McWilliams, professor of women's studies at Portland State University. "As a hallmark of Maoist China, the revolutionary impulse to eradicate previous styles of dress, and especially those deemed bourgeois and feminine, and in their place promote a desexualized uniform became a key strategy to challenge and displace the trappings of gendered forms of class inequality."[37] In other words, in its effort to generate a new labor force, the culture of Communist China selectively ignored gender differences in large part by avoiding "feminine" dress.

Modern Chinese women, however, see consumption and a carefully curated personal (and individual) sense of style as a sign of cosmopolitanism, and even as a positive step into participation in the Chinese socialist market economy. Put another way, whereas under Mao worldly fashion and femininity were threats to the new state, today these same concerns are interpreted as contributions. Dressing well means support of the project of China joining the world economy, continuing to grow into a major power. Says McWilliams,

> These young women build their sense of gendered and sexual identity through the consumption of products that rely on and produce a heightened performance of femininity. Responding to the call to consume as the action of a responsible post-socialist citizen, many young women go happily along the fashionable corridors of cosmetics and clothing displays enacting their good cultural citizenship by shopping to produce a state-sanctioned femininity.[38]

In terms of body modesty, Chinese women are the opposite of Indian ones: legs, all the way up, are fine to show in public, but breasts are usually hidden. According to blogger Becky Ances, a writer and teacher living in Xiamen, Chinese girls "wear the teeny tiniest shorts, yet rarely show cleavage. . . . If a girl wears tiny, tiny shorts, or a tiny, tight skirt that is shorter than her shirt, she's not showing off. In fact, many of my college students who have never kissed a boy wear tiny shorts or skip the pants altogether and wear just leggings."[39]

When Westerners think of Chinese women, we also often think of the practice of foot-binding, in which girls' feet are bound with strips of cloth to cause them to grow unnaturally. This was done to upper-class girls to make them more marriageable, because the mincing steps of a woman with four-inch feet were considered very feminine and attractive. Moreover, there was an implicit connection with wealth: only the wealthiest woman could afford the servants and staff necessary to make the use of her own feet optional, and wealthy men could communicate their standing by having a wife who was visibly kept. This practice falls under the heading of body modification rather than clothing, but its function is the same: to present a body that telegraphs something specific—such as status or power—via the skillful adherence to cultural rules about beauty.

Many of us in the West point to the practice of foot-binding and shake our heads, much the same way we do when we see a woman in hijab. (Please note that though the practice of foot-binding ended one hundred years ago, it still seems to capture the Western imagination.) But how is foot-binding that different from the body alterations performed by many wealthy American women (or, for that matter, high heels)? Yes, foot-binding took longer, as it is a process that extended through the years in which girls grew into adulthood. But the point was to communicate wealth and social standing by intimating that the woman in question could *afford* not to work—she was so sure she would never need to (or, more accurately, her family wanted her to be so sure) that her feet were rendered almost totally useless.

In the same way, many women spend hours getting manicures or eyelash and hair extensions, alterations that, by their very nature, prevent women from exerting ourselves and ensure that we must spend time or energy every day tending to these additions. These are not permanent alterations, of course, but they do impart a high status "kept-ness" to a woman's appearance. And some of us *do* alter our bodies permanently: Chinese girls had their feet bound with strips of cloth, and modern women receive injections to our faces; we allow surgeons to cut into our bodies with scalpels and sew us back up with a needle and thread; we sit for hours with toxic chemicals on our heads. And as an avid chemical sitter, I can attest that some of that stuff is actually enjoyable. Not physically, but it makes us feel as though we're performing womanhood correctly. There's a security in jumping through those hoops, bizarre though they ultimately are.

LESS CLOTHING, MORE MODIFICATION

Clothing is one way to connote social value, but in environments in which there is simply less clothing to be worn, messages about power or status are sometimes written on the skin. For example, the Tiv of northern Nigeria have been studied extensively for their intricate uses of scarification (the intentional infliction of scars).

For Tiv women, a series of concentric dashes, emanating outward from the navel, tells the story of her lineage and predicts the successful continuation of that lineage into the future. These scars are induced at puberty and, writes anthropologist John W. Burton, "may take twenty-five years to complete."[40] Adult women literally have the history of their families written on their bellies; children do not. This means that scarification is a rite of passage into adulthood and a physical indication of maturational status, perhaps analogous to the difference between the way an eight-year-old Western girl might dress and the way an eighteen-year-old might. Also from Burton, "Tiv women regard these scars as both signs of fertility and the promise of its realization."[41] Tiv men are also scarred, and one woman explained, "Of course it is painful. What woman would look at a man if his scars had not cost him pain?"[42]

Initiation into adulthood is often marked by physical modification—but what's particularly relevant to this discussion is how gender is constructed and reinforced within these rituals. On the island of Wogeo (one of the Schouten Islands off the coast of Papua New Guinea), women are thought of as "inherently superior physical beings in comparison to men. Menstruation is regarded as a natural feminine process that habitually purifies women from their contact with men."[43] To say that again, in nonacademic speak: women bleed every month to cleanse themselves of the weakening influence of men. How's *that* for a different framework for a woman's period?

Men, when they hit puberty, are taught by their fathers to ritually pierce and scarify their tongues; additionally, they are taught to "menstruate" in order to cleanse themselves of impurities, since their bodies do not do so naturally. A man wades out into shallow water and, writes British anthropologist Ian Hogbin, "covers his head with a palm spathe, . . . induces an erection, . . . pushes back the foreskin and hacks at the glans, first on the left side, then on the right. . . . He waits till the cut is dry and the sea is no longer pink and then walks to shore. After wrapping his penis in leaves, he dresses and goes back to the village."[44]

The Kayapo, a native tribe of the southern edge of the Amazon rain forest, have intricate customs involving hair, body paint, and piercing that serve as cultural signifiers, even though they wear almost nothing. Cultural anthropologist Terence S. Turner writes,

A well turned out adult Kayapo male, with his large lower-lip plug (a saucer-like disc some six centimetres across), penis sheath (a small cone made of palm leaves covering the *glans penis*), large holes pierced through the ear lobes from which hang small strings of beads, overall body paint in red and black patterns, plucked eyebrows, eyelashes and facial hair, and head shaved to a point at the crown with the hair left long at the sides and back, could . . . hardly leave the most insensitive traveller with the impression that bodily adornment is a neglected art among the Kayapo.[45]

Each element of adornment mentioned above has a specific cultural purpose. The penis sheath is bestowed when a young boy is deemed ready for sexual activity. It is meant to prevent public erections: "A public erection, or even the publicly visible protrusion of the glans penis through the foreskin without erection, is as embarrassing for a Kayapo male as walking naked through one's town or work place would be for a Westerner. It is the action of the sheath in preventing such an eventuality that is the basis of its symbolic meaning," says Turner.[46] The strings of beads in the ears have to do with the way in which the Kayapo conceptualize language and understanding: those with beads, as opposed to the plugs, which are worn by babies, have demonstrated the ability to speak and understand language and therefore can live as social beings among their peers.

The lip-ring references the hierarchy among the Kayapo, which is understood as a political hierarchy: public, blustery speaking in the men's communal house is a mark of seniority and dominance, and as "the essential medium of political power," speaking or chanting is referenced by the size of a man's lip disc.[47] When a man ages and retires from political life, or stops making as many decisions within the tribe, he may decrease the size of his lip plug, or he may adopt an heirloom plug, made from milky white stone. These "most precious and prestigious object[s] in the entire Kayapo wardrobe" may be passed down for generations.[48]

In the more remote Kayapo tribes where Western clothing is not worn, the bodies of men, women, and children are elaborately painted in red and black. In yet another social boundary between childhood and adulthood, children are painted in a completely different way than adults are. Black, the word for which also refers to the area just outside the village through which one passes on the way to the forest, "is associated with the idea of transformation between society and unsocialised nature"[49]—to use an imperfect analogy, it symbolizes the space between the id and the superego. Black paint is applied to the areas of the body "conceived to be the seat of its 'natural' powers and energies (the trunk, internal and reproductive organs, major muscles, etc.) that are in themselves beyond the reach of socialization."[50] The application of black, then, is meant to keep the individual's energy from causing him or her to transgress socially. Red, on the other hand, is associated with vitality and intensification, so it is applied to the parts of the body that help an individual get along in the world around him or her: the hands, feet, and especially the face.

This keen sensitivity to the body as social canvas is particularly visible in how they treat the subject of hair. The Kayapo are extremely clean, bathing at least once a day, and the plucking of body and facial hair is a way of enacting "this same fundamental principle of transforming the skin from a mere 'natural' envelope of the physical body into a sort of social filter."[51] The hair on one's head is so important for delineating cultural identity that, generally among Central Brazilian tribes, how one wears one's hair is the principal way of telling the peoples apart.

If even those who wear little clothing use their bodies to communicate social meaning, it would be silly to suggest that there's a way to avoid doing so here in the United States. Human beings, wherever we are, wear what Turner calls a "social skin." This is not to say that the trappings of such are universal: between veiled men and women draped in cloth, menstruating men and children painted from head to toe, it's hard to imagine that the American Suit represents any kind of universal truth instead of one set of customs, among many, meant to connote one particular set of cultural values.

So if the Suit is so arbitrary, why are Western women made to feel like it's a matter of life and fucking death?

MOUNTAIN VIEW, CALIFORNIA, 2016

I need an allergist. Yes, I was aware that I was allergic to cats, but when we got married, I was not going to ask my husband to get rid of his two non-hypoallergenic kitties. So here I am, on a rainy day, at Dr. H's office, my nose clogged and my face itchy.

I was unaware that sometimes allergists perform minor plastic surgery, like giving Botox injections and doing microdermabrasions. I have vowed never even to enter a plastic surgeon's office, not because I'm just that empowered but because I am secretly afraid I'd be tempted.

I am thirty-four, and I have noticed that my self-righteous refusal to even consider plastic surgery began to slip when I noticed my "marionette lines"—those lines that go straight down from the sides of your nose, past your lips, and partition your once-youthful chin into a weird, old-lady knob. They make me look fat. I do not like it, but I have never been to an actual plastic surgeon before. Now that I am in the office of someone who combats aging medically, I am amazed at the options I have. *Maybe I could just fix the marionette lines and not tell anyone*, I think. I immediately chastise myself, but the thought never totally goes away. Finally, my name is called.

After she's completed my exam, Dr. H explains that I need to have my tonsils removed. "You'll need to take about a week off," she explains. "And you'll need heavy painkillers. This operation is harder for adults than for kids, so be prepared not to eat any solids for at least a week."

Suddenly she brushes my bangs back. "What are you doing for skin care?" she asks abruptly.

I am immediately self-conscious. "Uh . . . I've been wearing sunscreen every day since I was fifteen," I say. I'm assuming she's wondering about my persistent acne up there, of which I am still ashamed, but after the Experiment, I hardly cover up anymore. Then she says, "You're starting to get some lines up here. Do you have an antiaging regime?"

There's something wrong with my forehead *now? My fucking* forehead*?!*

"No, no antiaging," I stammer. "Just soap and sunscreen."

She proceeds to try to sell me an outrageously expensive skincare line, mentioning that my neck could use some tightening too.

I am so angry that I vow never to go back. And I don't. Not because I'm insulted but because I really did not need to hear, from a medical professional, that I'm deficient. That was, to put it finely, shitty. *I bet men can just get healthcare without being told they need "tightening,"* I think as I leave. I don't bother to research whether or not that's true.

It's natural to think of one's own cultural practices as normative and to view others' as different or even weird. After all, humans long ago evolved not in tandem with survival concerns but in ways conducive to group coherence. So, of course the Suit seems like an imperative.

But it's not. It's just a costume, and it's *100 percent* arbitrary.

Which, when you actually think about it, changes everything. I would know: nothing has been the same since I took off the Suit, even after I put it back on.

NOW WHAT?

WASHINGTON, DC, JANUARY 21, 2017

It's 6:30 a.m., and I'm wide awake. I have been awake pretty much all night, since I got in at 2 a.m. I am too nervous to sleep. From my spot on the couch, I can see the sky turning purple through the small basement window. It's gray, but not raining. *That's good*, I think. *Nothing worse than being wet* and *angry*.

At seven, my friend Terry, whom I've come to call my honorary little brother after twenty years of friendship, and his wife, Amy, wander out of their bedroom. Amy, a brilliant young woman with perpetually perfect eyeliner, has been to many protests in her life. She warns me to bring a handkerchief in case of tear gas. "It really does help," she explains. Terry, who has spent a lot of time overseas as a member of the Special Forces, agrees, although his situation is different: because he has security clearance, he must wear a mask at all times or risk losing his job.

The three of us, plus their roommate Tom and his boyfriend, eat eggs and waffles together before piling into Terry's car. Tom's boyfriend leaves for work, and I comment that our little group sounds like the setup for a joke: a gay guy, a pastor, a social justice activist, and a soldier go to protest the patriarchy . . .

We drive from Terry's house in the DC suburbs to the last stop on the subway line into town. So many people are trying to get Metro tickets that we wonder if we should try another line, but a cheer erupts from a hundred women in pink pussy hats as the gate agent simply opens the turnstile and tells us to pay when we get off downtown. He smiles at us and wishes us luck as we pass the booth.

With the exception of some guy on the train who's convinced that the Metro agent asking him to move farther into the car is trying to make him "crush kids" (his daughter and wife are in the space he's created, while his friend brushes his crotch against my butt in the age-old insecure-male expression for "All space is my space"), everyone is incredibly polite. We emerge from the station into a gray morning, and at first, there's room to walk.

Everyone is moving in the same direction, and along the route, street vendors have set up stations with T-shirts saying, "Pussy grabs back" and "Dump Trump." After half a mile the crowd is much thicker, and as the dome of the Capitol rises down the street, a chant emerges: "Show me what a feminist looks like?" *This is what a feminist looks like!*" we holler back with gusto.

Terry, Amy, and I are actively trying to find the starting point for the march, but of course, our cell phones are struggling as so many people try to use the network. Soon it becomes clear that there will be no actual marching, just standing and wandering. It's too crowded to go from point A to point B.

I have never in my life seen this many people. There are tall brown men with rounded Afros, sixtysomething white women, young girls in colorful socks and fairy wings. It occurs to me suddenly that if anyone panics or even sets off a smoke bomb, we have nowhere to go. I'm struck by how volatile this situation could be. I think of Less, how his father was once shot in the leg, marching for his rights as a black man. Less knows spaces like these better than I do; he knows just how quickly they can go bad. But in truth, I'm not that worried: it would be unseemly for the cops to treat a huge group of mostly white women the way they too often treat large groups of black people.

But it just never gets there. The strongest words are said by a woman onstage who I presume is an activist: "Donald Trump can *suck* a *dick!*" (lots of cheering, including from me) and "I have thought an awful lot about *blowing up the White House*" (many groans and discomfort from the crowd on that one). We couldn't see the stage, so we didn't find out until we checked the news later that it was Madonna who'd been speaking.

At one point, we are all wandering in a sort of easterly direction (I could tell that, like me, most of the protestors had never been to DC, because we had no idea where we were going). An ambulance makes its way slowly through the crowd. A man in riot gear climbs to the roof of the cab and a hush falls over the street.

Is this it? Will they fire tear gas at us? Tell us to disperse or be arrested? Will we get hurt?

Whatever it is, we are ready. He lifts a megaphone.

"Can I have your attention, please?" he intones. With thousands of eyes on him, he points to the west. "The march . . . is *that way.*"

Everyone cheers, relieved, and changes direction as one.

Before the election, I asked myself, "Will we still need this book when we have a female president?" I should have seen the election of Donald Trump coming, though. *Especially* after the Experiment.

For those of us privileged enough to believe the United States has moved past much of its misogyny and racism, Trump's election was a shock. White progressives, like me, didn't honestly believe we still had so far to go as a country. Brown folks, of course, said, "Nothing is different, except now the hate is out in the open."

In the same way, taking off the Suit showed me the truth about how far US culture has yet to go. Please don't misunderstand: I hadn't magically transcended the limitations of modern womanhood just because I looked plain for almost a year. But the Suit had been my bulwark against feeling powerless, and after the Experiment the Suit felt like . . . not a joke exactly, but like I had been fighting all my battles with a foam sword, and everyone knew it but me. Once I realized what it really was—a poor substitute for safety or power—I couldn't go back. Perhaps this realization about the true nature of the Suit is something that happens with age anyway, but for me, the transition was stark, and disorienting.

When I would spend an hour on my hair post-Experiment, the way I did before, I would notice how anxious I was about stupid stuff like why the back was still wavy despite blow-drying it. I would ask myself, "Why are you so upset about this?" Putting on makeup to go out became a chore, not a joy, because it no longer felt aspirational. I wasn't thinking, "I'm gonna get that smoky eye like Charlize"; I was thinking, "I have to wear a ton of makeup to this event, but what if I do it wrong? Will the women I see be thinking, 'What a loser'?" I hate to use such a cliché, but I'd pulled back the curtain and the wizard was just a tiny guy from Kansas, and as the saying goes, you can't unsee what's been seen.

I dyed my hair pink, then purple; then I cut it all off. I found that I no longer lay awake at night thinking about whatever look I would go for the next day, saving me a lot of anxiety. On the other hand, when I had spare time, it was fun occasionally to get made up; when it felt like my choice, I enjoyed it. I still liked going to my salon, reveling in the smell of warm hair products and the sounds of women talking to each other in that way we do when there are no straight men around, but I no longer go hoping that I will look totally different when I emerge. I still treasure the fragrances Mom and I buy together at the mall when I visit her—I am wearing one now, in fact. It makes me feel loved.

For the first time in my life and for several years, I found that I didn't know what my personal style or my look were. This may sound silly to some, but for me it was like waking up in the middle of nowhere, with no idea where I was or how I'd gotten there. I had a bunch of new internal space to fill, and that was strange at first.

For a while, I considered whether I should just go full-modest again. After all, one criticism I got from other feminists was that I had only gone modest to get attention and then conveniently had gone back to looking conventional. But I couldn't think of a compelling reason, unless I was doing a project like the Experiment, to be that extreme about modesty anymore. My faith doesn't require it; my faith requires me to engage critically with the values the world espouses (consumerism, white supremacy, heteropatriarchy), but it does not ask me to hide myself. Covering completely now feels inauthentic to me.

I have to admit, this new headspace is not entirely pleasant. The Suit gave me a false sense of empowerment, but now I *see* the tiny jabs aimed at women rather than just feeling them as before. I am angrier now. But I suspect I was angry before; I had just learned to beautify my way out of facing it. Without the Suit there's nothing to fill the gap between how liberated I'm told I am and my actual experience, and that void is hard to look at, and even harder to live with. It's especially taxing to explain to some men that my version of feminism has nothing at all to do with them, one way or the other, neither privileging their perspectives nor hating them simply because they're male. That seems to anger some people greatly.

Taking off the costume—the one for my supporting role for guys—was the first step in getting off the stage of male centrality, and that's been disorienting. Once I began to notice how often men demanded my time and emotional energy simply because I was female, I became infinitely less patient with the process of tending to their egos. In 2016, before my pastor had to leave California due to housing prices and asked me to step into a role I would come to know as my calling, I briefly had a job in a small film company run by a man in his fifties. Most of the employees were young women (really young, like still in undergrad) who wore yoga pants to the office and who knew absolutely nothing about filmmaking. The producer never hit on me, but he didn't seem to understand why I got angry when he listened to my ideas only when his male employees spoke them. (It became a joke between me and a male coworker with whom I became friends: if I wanted to get something done, I had to ask my friend to suggest it.) He sat too close to his nineteen-year-old accounting manager on the couch and once told her she smelled "delicious." When he showed me the music video he'd made where his female employees danced in little black dresses and six-inch heels while he stood there in a tux, I didn't even give two weeks' notice.

On the other hand, I notice, to my dismay, how often I automatically fall into a role of protecting men from any discomfort. I do it with Less, even though he's never demanded such labor from me. I often sacrifice my time alone—which I prize, as an introvert—without him asking, in order to be sure I am available to him at all times. That's a constant battle for me. I also protected some of the parishioners I served: when they would tell me I was more fun to look at than most pastors, I would smile and thank them. (When I take my next church job, I'll give a kind but clear speech about what is and is not OK to say to a female pastor.) At the boxing gym I attend, if a male trainer and the female manager are standing next to each other, I will often choose to address the guy, no matter the subject.

Mostly, though, I find that the Suit no longer feels like an extension of me. Instead it's just a tool. What it does when I put it on is predictable. That is way, way less fun than believing that how I look, which is easy to change, is the same as who I am inside—but knowing the true nature of the Suit does make me feel stronger. Genuinely, irreducibly, Wonder Womanly stronger.

When that audiotape of Trump in 2005 surfaced ("I better use some Tic Tacs just in case I start kissing her. You know, I'm automatically attracted to beautiful— I just start kissing them. It's like a magnet. Just kiss. I don't even wait. And when you're a star, they let you do it. You can do anything. . . . Grab 'em by the pussy. You can do anything."[1]), it felt like the nail in the coffin of his pursuit of the presidency. But it wasn't.

We know, now, that much of America is invested in—not only accepts but is actively invested in—the idea that misogyny is an acceptable part of Western culture. If we as individuals do not believe this, then we must take steps to get out from under it, because apparently the electoral process won't help us. Fortunately, we don't have to march or make speeches to do this. We can make tiny changes and see where they lead.

If you're a woman who's been reading this book and thinking "I could never go out without makeup," this list of actions is for you. Try one, a few, or all of these:

1. *Reclaim your time.*
   Tack up a sheet of paper next to your mirror. (This exercise is also a great excuse to make a new page in your bullet journal, if you're into that kind of thing.) Then, document how much time you spend daily on the Suit for one week. Makeup and hair, yes, but if you go to the gym or do meal prep to stay slim, add that too. (There is a difference between working out to be healthy and working out to fit into the Suit, and only you know which you do. It probably changes from day to day.) Include shopping, if it's for enhancing or altering the Suit. At the end of the week, add it all up.
   This information is not meant to be a judgment but merely an accounting of how much time you invest, voluntarily or otherwise, on making yourself "acceptable." You're trying to show yourself your own life and asking yourself if you like what you see. Think of it like a food log: you'll be amazed by how much time the Suit consumes. Are you in control of the Suit or is it in control of you?

2. *Go without makeup for a day.*
   If this feels impossible for you, that's why you should absolutely do it. If you work in the service industry you may have to wear makeup, but then again, even female pastors get told they need to wear more makeup by their parishioners. So whatever. If you can, go to work or out with friends barefaced. Go someplace where people will see you—don't just stay home. If you like, get a group of girlfriends and support one another while you're out.

Someone, a coworker or friend, may ask if you're feeling OK. Shake it off; they're showing concern, and that's kind. Think of how dudes get to come to work without makeup and how no one ever tells them they look tired. Remember that part of the reason you look different to people is that you've always worn makeup when you see them.

Notice the reactions, especially if the person who speaks up about how you look is a guy. If you feel comfortable enough, tell him what you're doing. If he reacts with incredulity or mansplaining, this is a huge gift to you: note how powerful his response is. Why would he care what you put on your face? Why does it matter to him?

Ask yourself, at the end of the day, how *you* felt about it. Was it awful? Freeing? Did you feel ugly or prettier? Did you not feel any difference? Whatever you feel is fine. The point is to check in with yourself, rather than just doing what you think you must do because of the social pressure to wear the Suit. It may be earth-shattering; it may be NBD. The point is, you did it. What does that mean to you?

3. *Take a weeklong hiatus from social media.*
   If you don't need to be on social media for work—like, you're not in marketing—tell your Friends list that you're taking a week off. If you feel the need, clarify that it's not because you don't care what's going on in the world, but that you need to get your head right. Stay off everything you reach for when you feel bored or when you feel that itch for attention.

   The point is to cultivate the habit of knowing when you feel the urge to self-objectify and to name it for yourself. Then you can ask yourself what's making you do this, how you're feeling in that moment, and whether

there's something else you might do that might be better
for your well-being.

Again, try not to judge yourself if you struggle with
this. The idea is to get more in touch with your inner
voice, so that you can be self-directed, not driven by
endless Likes and Retweets. The point is *intentional
engagement* with social media instead of knee-jerk time-
line scrolling. At the end of your week, ask yourself how
you feel.

4. *Notice other women in the Suit and appreciate them.*
   Acknowledging and supporting other women is a basic
   part of being a feminist. The world can be shitty to women.
   Don't ever, ever make it shittier, even if you don't like what
   another woman is doing (unless she's saying or doing racist
   nonsense, in which case if you're both white, you need to
   come get your people). In the course of learning about
   your own Suit, don't judge other women for theirs.

   Instead, look for the ways the women around you
   craft their Suits. They're often creative, and usually
   time-consuming. If you know these women well, think
   about how their Suit interacts with their lives, why they
   would choose to wear the Suit they do. For example, if
   your girlfriend is a lawyer, think about how she has to
   rock those heels in the courtroom because of what they
   communicate. Perhaps ask her if, given the choice, she
   would wear sheep slippers instead. Maybe, maybe not: she
   might feel like a badass when she's towering over the
   opposition, or she might wish she could burn those things
   at the end of the day.

5. *Notice how often female power is conflated with sex appeal in
   the media.*
   Once you start paying attention to how the media
   portrays female power, you'll notice it absolutely

everywhere. The modern world demands media literacy, and engaging critically with the messages presented to us is vital to our mental health. Notice how often a woman portrayed as sexy is shorthand for "powerful." You'll be amazed by how often it shows up.

6. *If you have the lady stones, do your own Experiment for a week—or longer if you're nasty.*
You can cover your hair if you want to, but it's pretty hard to justify such a huge change without it coming off as inauthentic, especially if you're not religious. I recommend for a set period of time going barefaced, covering to the elbow and knee, and not wearing anything that makes you suck it in. See how you feel. If you have a good friend group, tell them about it; they may even want to join in.

It took me about two weeks to get comfortable with the idea that I looked fine, thanks, without makeup and covered, but I know that some women would only want to do a week. I would say, though, give it as much time as you can. It'll suck, and then it'll be fine, and then you'll forget all about it and you'll wonder why you thought the Suit was so vital to your existence.

You may notice, as I did, that certain people cease to see you. Think about what this might mean. I believed it had to do with the Suit connoting voluntary participation in popular culture (with all the objectification that entails), but it may mean something different to you.

The point of all these small, individual exercises is to make yourself uncomfortable, because discomfort is necessary for change. The Suit makes women OK with the amount of bullshit we're expected to tolerate just because of the bodies we're born in, and it's not OK. So try feeling weird. I promise, it will change your perspective. It might change it in ways that are painful. Be ready.

Taking off the Suit hurt, but it also woke me up. Women shouldn't be expected to do everything men do but backward and in heels, only to be told that unless our hair looks perfect while we do it and we never make men feel rejected and we *never* get mad, it isn't worth anything; and by the way, if a man assaults us, it's somehow our fault.

Life is too short to keep cramming ourselves into a costume that tells us we're secondary in the world. We bear kids, we advance in the workforce even as we endure harassment, we still do most of the housework even though we also work full-time. All over the world we're shouted at and assaulted and demeaned, and we still get up every day and get shit done, and just because we look OK doing it doesn't mean we feel OK. The Suit is no longer enough.

We've outgrown it; we deserve a new model of empowerment. It's time.

ACKNOWLEDGMENTS

This is my first book, and I'm not exaggerating when I say that it absolutely wouldn't have happened if I hadn't had the support of the following people. First, my agent, Sarah Levitt at Aevitas Creative Management, who has always had faith in me and had the kindness and wisdom to guide a pseudo-reluctant, first-time writer through a process that most authors are already familiar with by the time they get to the stage where I found myself at. Knowing I had someone so competent in my corner gave me confidence on the days I had none. My editor, Amy Miller Caldwell, immediately got what I was trying to do with the project, which meant I felt both supported and listened to. I'm humbled that a publishing house that stands for so much saw something in my work. Michelle Valigursky took an interest in my project when I was still a student and pointed me in the direction of my first agent, Chelsea Gilmore. Thanks are also due to both of them for their encouragement and faith. Thanks also to Linda Loewenthal at the David Black Agency for her helpful notes on my manuscript. Thanks to Sarah Hepola, who published the infamous *Salon* article that unexpectedly launched my career, and to Suzanne Van Atten, who led the writers' group that tolerated my floundering as I tried to figure out, belatedly, how to write something more than a single article that other people would want to read. Jerry Wang brought out my good side in pictures, a process that could have been extremely awkward but was instead a joy. Thanks are also due to my dad, Charles J. Shields, who inadvertently (maybe) made me into a writer, and who continues to help me anticipate what will be expected of me in the world of professional publishing. Dad, you're an invaluable source of encouragement, and so much more.

Sarah Maeve, Charmaine, Ella, Anna-Lee, Sarah M.S., Carrie, and Simi: Thank you for sharing your perspectives about the Suit with me. I needed your voices to help ground me. Thanks to Matt M. I'm sorry things turned out the way they did, but thank you for your encouragement anyway. Noël, you held my makeup and my tether to reality, even when I lost it for a while. Thank you for loving me even when I was a mess. Thanks also to my cosmic dad, Jay, who utterly changed my life. A couple of times. To Jess, who's known me since we were twelve and whose commitment to the art of friendship has loved me back into wholeness more times than I can count. I'm so lucky to have the love of someone so remarkable. To Rajah, who keeps me accountable and inspires me to be better, you're a pretty awesome person. Thank you for introducing me to your dad. I promise I'll take good care of him.

To Mom, who showed me that no matter what, people are going to be threatened by any woman with a brain, a sense of humor, an education, or all three, so you might as well kick ass and see who applauds and who complains. Nothing makes me happier than when people say, "You're just like your mom!"

To Less . . . I don't know how I ended up with someone so perfectly equipped to help me through the process of writing a potentially controversial book, but I did. I would have given up on this long ago if not for you, and I mean that. And if you say, "I told you you could do it," I'm gonna smack you. I mean that too.

NOTES

INTRODUCTION: WOMEN CAN DO ANYTHING—NO, NOT *THAT*

1. Jeanette C. and Robert H. Lauer, "A Case Study: The Bloomer Costume," in *Dress and Identity*, ed. Mary Ellen Roach-Higgins, Joanne B. Eicher, Kim K. P. Johnson (New York: Fairchild Productions, 1995), 406.

2. Jennifer Lee, "Feminism Has a Bra-Burning Myth Problem," *Time*, June 12, 2014, http://time.com/2853184/feminism-has-a-bra-burning-myth-problem/.

3. Joel Stein, "Nip. Tuck. Or Else: Why You'll Be Getting Cosmetic Procedures Even If You Don't Want To," *Time*, June 29, 2015.

4. Terence Blacker, "Kristin Scott Thomas, Embrace Your New Role as the Invisible Woman—We All Disappear as We Age," *Independent*, July 29, 2013, http://www.independent.co.uk/voices/comment/kristin-scott-thomas-embrace-your-new-role-as-the-invisible-woman-we-all-disappear-as-we-age-8736607.html.

CHAPTER 1: KATY PERRY IN A LEOPARD BUSTIER

1. Ariel Levy, *Female Chauvinist Pigs: Women and the Rise of Raunch Culture* (New York: Free Press, 2005), 105.

2. Brit Harper and Marika Tiggemann, "The Effect of Thin Ideal Media Images on Women's Self-Objectification, Mood, and Body Image," *Sex Roles* 58 (2008): 649–57, doi: 10.1007/s11199–007–9379-x.

3. Peggy Orenstein, *Cinderella Ate My Daughter: Dispatches from the Frontlines of the New Girlie-Girl Culture* (New York: HarperCollins, 2011), 79.

4. Stephen Rodrick, "Serena Williams: The Great One," *Rolling Stone*, June 18, 2013, http://www.rollingstone.com/culture/news/serena-williams-the-great-one-20130618.

5. Jennifer Keishin Armstrong and Heather Wood Rudúlph, *Sexy Feminism: A Girl's Guide to Love, Success, and Style* (New York: Houghton Mifflin Harcourt, 2013), 1.

6. Ibid., 68.

7. Orenstein, *Cinderella Ate My Daughter*, 17.

8. Armstrong and Rudúlph, *Sexy Feminism*, xviii.

9. Ibid.

10. Aída Hurtado, *Voicing Chicana Feminisms:Young Women Speak Out on Sexuality and Identity* (NewYork: NewYork University Press, 2003), 184.

11. Alida Nugent, *You Don't Have to Like Me: Essays on Growing Up, Speaking Out, and Finding Feminism* (NewYork: Penguin Publishing Group), loc. 1088 of 3148, Kindle.

12. Stephanie Foo, "The Fever," *Reply All*, episode 27, June 4, 2015, Gimlet Media, https://gimletmedia.com/episode/27-the-fever/.

13. Nugent, *You Don't Have to Like Me*, loc. 1103.

14. Rebecca Solnit, *Men Explain Things to Me* (Chicago: Haymarket Books, 2013), loc. 226–27 of 1410, Kindle.

15. Nicolas Kristof, "To End the Abuse, She Grabbed a Knife," *NewYork Times*, March 8, 2014, https://www.nytimes.com/2014/03/09/opinion/sunday/kristof-to-end-the-abuse-she-grabbed-a-knife.html.

16. *Miss Representation*, directed and produced by Jennifer Siebel Newsom (San Francisco: Girls' Club Entertainment, 2011), documentary film.

17. Astra Taylor, "How the Cult of Internet Openness Enables Misogyny," *Mother Jones*, April 10, 2014, http://www.motherjones.com/media/2014/04/open-internet-closed-to-women/.

18. Suzanne LaBarre, "Why We're Shutting Off Our Comments," *Popular Science*, September 24, 2013, http://www.popsci.com/science/article/2013–09/why-were-shutting-our-comments?src=SOC&dom=tw.

19. Dale G. Larson and Robert L. Chastain, "Self-Concealment: Conceptualization, Measurement, and Health Implications," *Journal of Social and Clinical Psychology* 9, no. 4 (1990): 439–55.

CHAPTER 2: "IS THIS REALLY ANY BETTER?"

1. Joanna Plucinska, "Study Says White Extremists Have Killed More Americans in the U.S.Than Jihadists Since 9/11," *Time*, June 24, 2015, http://time.com/3934980/right-wing-extremists-white-terrorism-islamist-jihadi-dangerous/.

2. Sumbul Ali-Karamali, *The Muslim Next Door:The Qur'an, the Media, and That Veil Thing* (Ashland, OR:White Cloud Press, 2008), 177.

3. Ibid., 122.

4. Ibid., 123.

5. Tariq Ramadan, *In the Footsteps of the Prophet: Lessons from the Life of Muhammad* (Oxford, UK: Oxford University Press, 2007), 34.

6. Mona Eltahawy, *Headscarves and Hymens:Why the Middle East Needs a Sexual Revolution* (NewYork: Farrar, Straus and Giroux, 2015), loc. 61 of 2633, Kindle.

7. Ibid., loc. 70.

8. Ibid., loc. 182.

9. Ibid., loc. 525.

10. Ibid., loc. 515.

11. Ibid., loc. 525.

12. Ali-Karamali, *The Muslim Next Door.*

13. Ibid.

14. Umm Adam, "I Do Care About Your Party," in *Women in Clothes*, ed. Sheila Heti, Heidi Julavits, and Leanne Shapton (New York: Penguin, 2014), 138.

15. Zinah Nur Sharif in conversation with Emma Tarlo, "Fashion Is the Biggest Oxymoron in My Life," in *Islamic Fashion and Anti-Fashion: New Perspectives from Europe and North America*, ed. Emma Tarlo and Annelies Moors (New York: Bloomsbury, 2013), 203.

16. Ibid., 205.

17. Edward W. Said, *Orientalism* (New York: Vintage Books, 1979), 3.

18. Rafia Zakaria, "Clothes and Daggers," *Aeon*, September 8, 2015, https://aeon.co/essays/ban-the-burqa-scrap-the-sari-why-women-s-clothing-matters.

19. "The Glass-Ceiling Index," *Economist*, March 7, 2013, http://www.economist.com/blogs/graphicdetail/2013/03/daily-chart-3.

CHAPTER 3: STILL NOT A NUN

1. Matthew Vines, "A Beloved Former Pastor Retracted His Support of Same-Sex Marriage. It Will Harm LGBTQ People More Than He May Know," *Time*, July 14, 2017, http://time.com/4859620/eugene-peterson-bible-homosexuality-gay-marriage/

2. "U.S. Public Becoming Less Religious," *Pew Forum*, November 3, 2015. http://www.pewforum.org/2015/11/03/chapter-3-views-of-religious-institutions.

3. John E. Newhagen, "TV News Images That Induce Anger, Fear, and Disgust: Effects on Approach/Avoidance and Memory," *Journal of Broadcasting and Electronic Media* 42, no. 2 (1998): 265–76.

4. "Starbucks Wanted to Take Christ and Christmas Off of Their Brand New Cups," *Washington Post* video, November 9, 2015, https://www.washingtonpost.com/video/national/starbucks-wanted-to-take-christ-and-christmas-off-of-their-brand-new-cups/2015/11/09/387fcd18-8703-11e5-bd91-d385b244482f_video.html.

5. Ed Stetzer, "When We Love Outrage More Than People: Starbucks Cups and You," *Christianity Today*, November 9, 2015, http://www.christianitytoday.com/edstetzer/2015/november/when-we-love-outrage-more-than-people-starbucks-cups-and-yo.html.

6. Joseph Campbell with Bill Moyers, *The Power of Myth* (New York: Anchor Books, 1991), 24.

7. Catherine Keller, *On the Mystery: Discerning Divinity in Process* (Minneapolis: Fortress Press, 2008), 10.

8. Bill T. Arnold and Bryan E. Beyer, *Readings from the Ancient Near East* (Grand Rapids, MI: Baker Academic, 2002), 15.

9. Anne McGrew Bennett, "Overcoming the Biblical and Traditional Subordination of Women," *Feminist Theological Ethics: A Reader* (Louisville, KY: Westminster John Knox Press, 1994), 137.

10. Ibid., 138.

11. Ibid.

12. Ibid.

13. Luke Timothy Johnson, *The Writings of the New Testament: An Interpretation* (Minneapolis: Fortress Press, 2010), 273.

CHAPTER 4: LESS G-STRING, MORE GUCCI

1. "Facts and Statistics: Did You Know?," Anxiety and Depression Association of America, September 2014, http://www.adaa.org/about-adaa/pressroom/facts-statistics; US Department of Health and Human Services, National Institutes of Health, National Institute of Mental Health, "Depression," NIH publication no. 15–3561 (Bethesda, MD: US Government Printing Office, 2015), http://www.nimh.nih.gov/health/publications/depression-what-you-need-to-know-12–2015/index.shtml#pub8; Franco Sassi, "How U.S. Obesity Compares with Other Countries," PBS.org, April 11, 2013, http://www.pbs.org/newshour/rundown/how-us-obesity-compares-with-other-countries/; Chris Arsenault, "Only 60 Years of Farming Left If Soil Degradation Continues," *Scientific American*, December 5, 2014, http://www.scientificamerican.com/article/only-60-years-of-farming-left-if-soil-degradation-continues/.

2. Oliver Milman, "Rate of Environmental Degradation Puts Life on Earth at Risk, Say Scientists," *Guardian*, January 15, 2015, https://www.theguardian.com/environment/2015/jan/15/rate-of-environmental-degradation-puts-life-on-earth-at-risk-say-scientists.

3. Emmanuel Saez, "Striking It Richer: The Evolution of Top Incomes in the United States (Updated with 2012 Preliminary Estimates)," paper, Department of Economics, University of California, Berkeley, September 3, 2013, http://eml.berkeley.edu/~saez/saez-UStopincomes-2012.pdf; Board of Governors of the Federal Reserve System, *Report of the Economic Well-Being of U.S. Households in 2014* (Washington, DC: Federal Reserve Board, May 2015), http://www.federalreserve.gov/econresdata/2014-report-economic-well-being-us-households-201505.pdf.

4. Elizabeth Kuhns, *The Habit: A History of the Clothing of Catholic Nuns* (New York: Doubleday, 2003), loc. 246 of 3284, Kindle.

5. Ibid., loc. 660.

6. Ibid., loc. 664.

7. Ibid.

8. Ibid., loc. 649.

9. Ibid., loc. 1084.

10. Ibid., loc. 303.

11. Timothy Fry, ed., *RB 1980: The Rule of St. Benedict in Latin and English with Notes* (Collegeville, MN: Liturgical Press, 1981), chap. 55.

12. Kuhns, *Habit*, loc. 374.

13. Ibid., loc. 1444.

14. Ibid., loc. 1217.

15. See *The Tertullian Project*, especially the section entitled "*De cultu feminarum* (On Female Fashion)," http://www.tertullian.org/works.htm.

16. Sara Harris, *The Sisters: The Changing World of the American Nun* (Indianapolis: Bobbs-Merrill, 1970), 28–29.

17. Charles E. Hurst and David L. McConnell, *An Amish Paradox: Diversity and Change in the World's Largest Amish Community* (Baltimore: Johns Hopkins University Press, 2010), loc. 414 of 7241, Kindle.

18. Stephen Scott, *Why Do They Dress That Way?* (Intercourse, PA: Good Books, 1997), 19.

19. Hurst and McConnell, *An Amish Paradox*, loc. 414.

20. Ibid., loc. 428.

21. Steven M. Nolt and Thomas J. Meyers, *Plain Diversity: Amish Cultures and Identities* (Baltimore: Johns Hopkins University Press, 2007), loc. 149 of 3024, Kindle.

22. "Amish Studies" homepage, Young Center for Anabaptist and Pietist Studies, Elizabethtown College, 2016, http://groups.etown.edu/amishstudies/.

23. Scott, *Why Do They Dress That Way?*, 12.

24. Sherry Gore, *The Plain Choice: A True Story of Choosing to Live an Amish Life* (Grand Rapids, MI: Zondervan, 2015), loc. 1838 of 2705, Kindle.

25. Scott, *Why Do They Dress That Way?*, 16.

26. Donald B. Kraybill, Karen M. Johnson-Weiner, and Steven M. Nolt, *The Amish* (Baltimore: Johns Hopkins University Press, 2013), loc. 2418 of 10781, Kindle.

27. Scott, *Why Do They Dress That Way?*, 24.

28. Kraybill, Johnson-Weiner, and Nolt, *The Amish*, loc. 3600.

29. Ibid., loc. 3654.

30. Ibid., loc. 2479.

31. Barry Schwartz, *The Paradox of Choice: Why More Is Less* (New York: Harper Collins, 2004).

32. Gore, *The Plain Choice*, loc. 1547.

33. Larissa Dzegar, "Exposed: The Gift of Virginity and Purity Balls," *Bust*, November 16, 2010, http://bust.com/tv/5793-exposed-the-gift-of-virginity-and-purity-balls.html.

34. Ben Protess, "Unearthing Exotic Provisions Buried in Dodd-Frank," *New York Times*, July 13, 2011, http://dealbook.nytimes.com/2011/07/13/unearthing-exotic-provisions-buried-in-dodd-frank/?_r=1; Marta Zaraska, *Meathooked: The History and Science of Our 2.5-Million-Year Obsession with Meat* (New York: Basic Books, 2016), 3.

35. International Labour Organization, *Marking Progress Against Child Labour: Global Estimates and Trends 2000–2012* (Geneva: International Labour Office/IPEC, 2013), http://www.ilo.org/global/topics/child-labour/lang—en/index.htm.

36. Gary Gardner, "Engaging Religions to Shape Worldviews," in *State of the World 2010: Transforming Cultures from Consumerism to Sustainability*, ed. Linda Starke and Lisa Mastny (London: Earthscan, 2010), 29, http://blogs.worldwatch .org/transformingcultures/wp-content/uploads/2009/04/Engaging-Religions -to-Shape-Worldviews-Gardner.pdf.

37. Zaraska, *Meathooked*, 3.

CHAPTER 5: TECH AND *TZNIUT*

1. Amazon.com summary of Nancy Jo Sales's *American Girls: Social Media and the Secret Lives of Teenagers*, https://www.amazon.com/American-Girls -Social-Secret-Teenagers/dp/0385353928.

2. Nancy Jo Sales, *American Girls: Social Media and the Secret Lives of Teenagers* (New York: Alfred A. Knopf, 2016), 25.

3. Ibid., 26.

4. Dian A. de Vries and Jochen Peter, "Women on Display: The Effect of Portraying the Self Online on Women's Self-Objectification," *Computers in Human Behavior* 29, no. 4 (2013): 1483–89, doi: 10.1016/j.chb.2013.01.015.

5. Kate Fagan, *What Made Maddy Run: The Secret Struggles and Tragic Death of an All-American Teen* (New York: Little, Brown, 2017), loc. 78 of 2954, Kindle.

6. Ibid., loc. 2129.

7. Ibid., loc. 430.

8. De Vries and Peter, "Women on Display," 1484–85.

9. Janis Wolak, Kimberly Mitchell, and David Finkelhor, "Unwanted and Wanted Exposure to Online Pornography in a National Sample of Youth Internet Users," *Pediatrics* 119 (2007): 247–57, http://www.unh.edu/ccrc/pdf /CV153.pdf.

10. "Social Media Fact Sheet," Pew Research Center, January 12, 2017, http://www.pewinternet.org/fact-sheet/social-media/.

11. National Institutes of Health, National Institute of Mental Health, "The Teen Brain: Still Under Construction," 2011, under "Health and Educa- tion: Publications," http://www.nimh.nih.gov/health/publications/the-teen -brain-still-under-construction/index.shtml.

12. Ibid.

13. American Psychological Association, *Report of the APA Task Force on the Sexualization of Girls* (Washington, DC: American Psychological Association, 2007), 20, http://www.apa.org/pi/women/programs/girls/report-full.pdf.

14. Deborah L. Tolman, *Dilemmas of Desire: Teenage Girls Talk About Sexuality* (Cambridge, MA: Harvard University Press, 2002), loc. 662 of 2819, Kindle.

15. Jacqueline Lunn, "Is Kim Kardashian Empowering?," MamaMia.com, April 1, 2016, http://www.mamamia.com.au/is-kim-kardashian-empowering/.

16. For examples, see Jaime Lutz, "N.C. Police Investigate Instagram Photos of Naked Teen Girls," *World News*, March 2, 2014, http://abcnews.go .com/blogs/headlines/2014/03/n-c-police-investigate-instagram-photos-of

-naked-teen-girls, and Michael Martinez, "Sexting Scandal: Colorado High School Faces Felony Investigation," CNN, November 9, 2015, http://www .cnn.com/2015/11/07/us/colorado-sexting-scandal-canon-city.

17. Louann Brizendine, *The Female Brain* (New York: Morgan Road Books, 2006), 32.

18. Yoree Koh, "Twitter's Diversity Report: Women Make Up 30% of Workforce," *Wall Street Journal*, July 23, 2014, https://blogs.wsj.com/digits /2014/07/23/twitters-diversity-report-women-make-up-30-of-workforce.

19. Stephanie Wellen Levine, *Mystics, Mavericks, and Merrymakers: An Intimate Journey Among Hasidic Girls* (New York: New York University Press, 2003), loc. 4077–86 of 5235, Kindle.

20. Ibid., loc. 2304.

21. Ibid., loc. 4091.

22. Ibid.

23. Barbara Goldman Carrell, "Shattered Vessels That Contain Divine Sparks: Unveiling Hasidic Women's Dress Code," in *The Veil: Women Writers on Its History, Lore, and Politics*, ed. Jennifer Heath (Berkeley: University of California Press, 2008), 50.

24. Ibid., 52.

25. Gila Manolson, *Outside/Inside: A Fresh Look at Tzniut* (Southfield, MI: Targum Press, 1995), 43.

26. Ibid., 20.

27. Amy K. Milligan, *Hair, Headwear, and Orthodox Jewish Women: Kallah's Choice* (Washington, DC: Lexington Books, 2014), loc. 1460–61 of 3459, Kindle.

28. Wendy Shalit, *The Good Girl Revolution: Young Rebels with Self-Esteem and High Standards* (New York: Ballantine Books, 2008), 26–27.

29. Debra Renee Kaufman, *Rachel's Daughters: Newly Orthodox Women* (New Brunswick, NJ: Rutgers University Press, 1991), loc. 621–25 of 2860, Kindle.

30. Psalm 45:14 (standard traditional Jewish version).

31. Levine, *Mystics, Mavericks, and Merrymakers*, loc. 950.

32. Leah Vincent, *Cut Me Loose: Sin and Salvation After My Ultra-Orthodox Girlhood* (New York: Penguin, 2014), 14.

33. Ibid., 17–18, 20.

34. Ibid., 44.

35. Leah Lax, *Uncovered: How I Left Hasidic Life and Finally Came Home* (Tempe, AZ: She Writes Press, 2015), 312.

CHAPTER 6: WORLDWIDE BEAUTY

1. Nina Sylvanus, "Fashionability in Colonial and Postcolonial Togo," in *African Dress: Fashion, Agency, Performance (Dress, Body, Culture)*, ed. Karen Tranberg Hansen and D. Soyini Madison (New York: Bloomsbury, 2013), 36.

2. Ibid.

3. M. Catherine Daly, Joanne B. Eicher, and Tonye V. Erekosima, "Male and Female Artistry in Kalabari Dress," in Roach-Higgins, Eicher, and Johnson, *Dress and Identity*, 340.

4. Misty L. Bastain, "Dressing for Success: The Politically Performative Quality of an Igbo Woman's Attire," in Hansen and Madison, *African Dress*, 15.

5. Ibid.

6. Sylvanus, "Fashionability in Colonial and Postcolonial Togo," 41.

7. Karen Tranberg Hansen, "Dressing Dangerously: Miniskirts, Gender Relations, and Sexuality in Zambia," in *Fashioning Africa: Power and the Politics of Dress*, ed. Jean Allman (Bloomington: Indiana University Press, 2004), 169.

8. Ibid., 171.

9. "Family Structure, Marriage and Kinship," *BedouinInfo* wiki, https://bedouininfo.wikispaces.com/Family+Structure+and+Kinship, accessed November 2016.

10. Lila V. Abu-Lughod, "The Romance of Resistance: Tracing Transformations of Power through Bedouin Women," in Roach-Higgins, Eicher, and Johnson, *Dress and Identity*, 165.

11. Henrietta Butler, *The Tuareg, or Kel Tamasheq: The People Who Speak Tamasheq* (Chicago: University of Chicago Press, 2015), 26.

12. Ibid., 32.

13. Ibid.

14. Ibid.

15. Arshie Qureshi, "I Was Told to Be Like a Lady First for Wearing Jeans," *Feminism in India*, February 9, 2016, http://feminisminindia.com/2015/02/09/be-like-a-lady.

16. Geetanjali Gangoli, *Indian Feminisms: Law, Patriarchies and Violence in India* (London: Routledge, 2016), 3.

17. Ibid., 7.

18. "Dressing the Indian Woman through History," *BBC News*, December 6, 2014, http://www.bbc.com/news/magazine-30330693.

19. Gardiner Harris, "After Life in New York, Banker Returns to India for Turn at Fashion," *New York Times*, September 14, 2012, http://www.nytimes.com/2012/09/15/world/asia/after-stint-in-new-york-banker-turns-to-fashion-in-india.html.

20. Ibid.

21. Ibid.

22. Rachel Jones, "The Do's and Don'ts of How to Dress in India," *Hippie in Heels* (blog), https://hippie-inheels.com/how-to-dress-in-india/, accessed November 8, 2017.

23. Kaori Shoji, "2016: The Year Japan Said 'Sayonara' to Some Sexist Terms," *Japan Times*, December 16, 2016, http://www.japantimes.co.jp/life/2016/12/26/language/2016-year-japan-said-sayonara-sexist-terms/#.WHQSmrYrJE7.

24. Chris Kincaid, "Gender Roles of Women in Modern Japan," *Japan Powered*, June 22, 2014, http://www.japanpowered.com/japan-culture/gender -roles-women-modern-japan.

25. Masami Ito, "Women of Japan Unite: Examining the Contemporary State of Feminism," *Japan Times*, October 3, 2015, http://www.japantimes.co .jp/life/2015/10/03/lifestyle/women-japan-unite-examining-contemporary -state-feminism/#.WHQY6LYrJE4.

26. Ibid.

27. Masafumi Monden, *Japanese Fashion Cultures: Dress and Gender in Contemporary Japan* (London: Bloomsbury, 2015), 78.

28. Ibid., 79.

29. Merry White, *The Material Child: Coming of Age in Japan and America* (Berkeley: University of California Press, 1994), 123, 185, quoted in Monden, *Japanese Fashion Cultures*, 96.

30. "The Glass-Ceiling Index," *Economist*, March 7, 2013, http://www .economist.com/blogs/graphicdetail/2013/03/daily-chart-3.

31. Jake Adelstein, "The Dubious Cost of Sexual Assault in Japan," *Japan Times*, November 5, 2016, http://www.japantimes.co.jp/news/2016/11/05 /national/media-national/dubious-cost-sexual-assault-japan/#.WHW_zLYrJE5.

32. "The Criminal Justice System: Statistics," RAINN.org, https://www .rainn.org/statistics/criminal-justice-system, accessed December 2016.

33. Xaiohe Xu, "The Prevalence and Determination of Wife Abuse in Urban China," *Journal of Comparative Family Studies* 28, no. 3 (Autumn 1997): 281.

34. Patricia Ebrey, "Women in Traditional China," Center for Global Education, http://asiasociety.org/education/women-traditional-china.

35. Xinyan Jiang, "The Dilemma Faced by Chinese Feminists," *Hypatia* 15, no. 3 (Summer 2000): 142.

36. Rong Chen, "Female Techs Excel in China's Aerospace Industry," January 10, 2017, All-China Women's Federation, http://www.womenofchina .cn/womenofchina/html1/features/spotlight/1701/1472-1.htm.

37. Sally E. McWilliams, "'People Don't Attack You If You Dress Fancy': Consuming Femininity in Contemporary China," *Women's Studies Quarterly* 41, nos. 1 and 2 (Spring–Summer 2013): 164.

38. Ibid., 167.

39. Becky Ances, "Figuring Out Chinese Modesty," September 16, 2013, http://www.beckyances.net/2013/09/figuring-out-chinese-modesty/.

40. John W. Burton, *Culture and the Human Body: An Anthropological Perspective* (Long Grove, IL: Waveland Press, 2001), 83.

41. Ibid., 84.

42. Ibid., 83.

43. Ibid., 77.

44. Ian Hogbin, *The Island of Menstruating Men: Religion in Wogeo, New Guinea* (Prospect Heights, IL: Waveland Press, 1970), 88–89.

45. Terence S. Turner, "The Social Skin," *HAU: Journal of Ethnographic Theory* 2, no. 2 (2012): 487, https://www.haujournal.org/index.php/hau/article/view/hau2.2.026/244.

46. Ibid., 490.

47. Ibid., 491.

48. Ibid., 492.

49. Ibid.

50. Ibid.

51. Ibid., 488.

CONCLUSION: NOW WHAT?

1. "Transcript: Donald Trump's Taped Comments About Women," *New York Times*, October 8, 2016, https://www.nytimes.com/2016/10/08/us/donald-trump-tape-transcript.html.